LESSONS
FROM THE
ROAD

LESSONS
FROM THE
ROAD

NIGEL JAMES WITH

THIRD DAY

Authentic

COLORADO SPRINGS • MILTON KEYNES • HYDERABAD

Authentic Publishing
We welcome your questions and comments.

USA   1820 Jet Stream Drive, Colorado Springs, CO 80921 www.authenticbooks.com
UK   9 Holdom Avenue, Bletchley, Milton Keynes, Bucks, MK1 1QR
      www.authenticmedia.co.uk
India Logos Bhavan, Medchal Road, Jeedimetla Village, Secunderabad 500 055, A.P.

Lessons from the Road
ISBN-13: 978-1-934068-48-9
ISBN-10: 1-934068-48-9

10 09 08 / 6 5 4 3 2 1

Published in 2008 by Authentic

Cover and interior design: projectluz.com
Editorial team: KJ Larson, Dan Johnson, Betsy Weinrich

Printed in the United States of America

TABLE OF CONTENTS

	Foreword	vii
1	Set This Place on Fire	1
2	Wanna Be a Rock Star	11
3	Come Together	31
4	Put Your Hand in Mine	49
5	Sing a Song	73
6	There Is Hope for the Helpless	93
7	Feels Like I'm a Million Miles Away	109
8	This Is the Body	131
9	Lord of All Creation	151
10	May Your Wonders Never Cease	171
	Copyright Info for Song Lyrics	187

FOREWORD

Not many people get the opportunity to travel in the cockpit of a Hercules transport plane during a night-flight from Tikrit to Baghdad in Iraq. In January 2008, I had the opportunity while on Third Day's *God and Country* tour to Kuwait and Iraq on a groundbreaking trip with USO to entertain American troops. Sitting behind the aircraft crew, I spent some time reflecting that we were the first contemporary Christian band to undertake a tour in a combat zone, and how in so many ways this short five-day tour encapsulated everything that was meaningful to the ministry of Third Day.

The apostle Paul often called believers traveling with him "fellow workers," but he also called them "fellow soldiers." What did Paul notice about soldiers that could be applied to living as Christians? I spent some time in our devotions paralleling characteristics of a soldier and a disciple: discipline, faithfulness, sacrifice, obedience, fellowship, conquering fear, vision, purpose. The military understands all of these. If you know how to live as a soldier, you know how to live as a Christian. The comradeship of the military, the "band of brothers," is something that Third Day aims for when we tour and we had plenty of role models in the people of faith we met in Iraq. Certain phrases from songs are intensified when you see them sung by a bunch of soldiers with arms raised and tears streaming down their faces.

We returned to Kuwait from Iraq on an "angel flight"—a plane carrying the casket of a fallen soldier. He paid the ultimate sacrifice; the sacrifices of a touring Christian rock band are trivial in comparison.

On our trip to Iraq, we learned much about ourselves and our faith. This book is simply about a band of brothers, fellow workers for the gospel, fellow soldiers of Christ, faithfully walking the path that the Lord Jesus has called us to follow. It is dedicated to fellow workers and fellow soldiers all over the world.

Nigel James, January 2008

1

SET THIS PLACE ON FIRE

—CONSUMING FIRE—

Set this place on fire
Send Your Spirit, Savior
Rescue from the mire
Show Your servant favor

MAC

From the beginning of Third Day we realized that we needed to have someone to speak into our lives as individuals and as a band. Through the years we have had many people, pastors, and friends travel with us. But of all those people, Nigel James has been the most important. He has allowed us and reminded us to be men of God first, and as a result, our music and ministry have reflected that. Nigel has kept us accountable to each other, to the church, and, of course, to our Lord. He has helped us to grow in our faith and has reminded us to stay focused on our calling and on what Third Day is really all about.

Mac Powell, November 2006

Whenever people find out that I travel with Third Day as their road pastor, they always ask me the same two questions. The second question is, "Do you need someone to carry your bags?" I laugh politely and mention that I'm strong enough to carry my own bags. However, the first question needs a more serious answer. Everyone always asks me, "How did you get the job of Third Day's road pastor?" Depending on how much time I have and how interested the person looks, I've got two possible replies. My short reply is that it is a "God thing"; and the longer reply, which explains the set of circumstances in which I've ended up working with the band, adds up to basically the same answer—it's a God thing.

If you think about the situation, it does seem to stretch the bounds of credibility that a man from Cardiff, Wales, in the UK would find himself in the privileged and responsible position of being spiritual adviser and friend to one of the most successful and influential bands in the history of Christian music. Equally unlikely is that their production manager would uproot from his home in Australia to join the band's crew, or that their merchandise manager is a missionary from Brazil. Yet that's the way God often works: "For just as the heavens are higher than the earth, so are my ways higher than your ways and my thoughts higher than your thoughts" (Isaiah 55:9 NLT). So let me explain how God orchestrated my relationship with Brad, David, Mac, Mark, and Tai.

It all started in the summer of 1995. My best friend, Gary Smith, and I had just left the employment of a national Christian youth organization in the UK to begin ministry together in a charity called Big Ideas (nothing to do with Veggie Tales!). For some years before this, we had been running a Christian music festival and had begun a friendship with the main guys in a Christian record company. Ian Hamilton, Dave Withers, and Dave Bruce, major players in the UK scene, started a new company called Alliance and needed some help developing live concerts and touring. They promised to send some opportunities our way when Gary and I set out together.

Our plan for the summer of 1995 was to leave our employment in June, spend July and early August on an evangelistic trip around youth camp sites, have a couple of weeks holiday late in August, and then officially begin ministry together in the first week of September.

Then two things happened that shaped my destiny: first, Gary got ill with a kidney stone and had to return home early from the evangelistic trip. In fact, he ended up in the hospital. Second, Alliance Music called us to ask if we could look after an American band that was coming over to the UK and Europe for a week. Basically they needed a minibus driver to take a band called Newsboys around the UK, Holland, and Germany.

I have to admit I'd never heard of them but had it on good authority that they were good and were gaining a great reputation. Already Gary and I had decided that he would do more of the management, events, and organizing and that I would do more speaking and evangelism. Had Gary been well, he would have driven Newsboys around, but because we couldn't turn down such a great opportunity, I found myself escorting them around when I thought I'd be having a few quiet days before starting a new ministry.

A week on the road with Newsboys was a blast and my first introduction to the nuts and bolts of the Christian music world. I'd been a fan of contemporary Christian music since I was a student in the late '70s and early '80s, but now I was experiencing it from the inside. Peter Furler and the rest of the guys of Newsboys really welcomed me, and we shared many plates of "pie and chips" during that week. Newsboys' management, Wes and Steve Campbell, became very good friends of mine, and Gary recovered enough to run a showcase concert for Alliance with Newsboys as top of the bill.

Over the next few years, Alliance Music flew Gary and me to the Gospel Music Association conference in Nashville, Tennessee, to find bands and performers who would relish the opportunity of playing in the UK. Each time we went to Nashville, we would stay with either Wes Campbell or Duncan Phillips, and we got to know Newsboys better and better. Peter Furler would often suggest that they bring me over to the US to work as the road manager, and I kept replying that I was a pastoral/speaker-type person, not a management dude! I must admit that my appetite for life on the road in the US was whetted on one occasion when I flew up from Nashville to Chicago to see

Newsboys perform at a Luis Palau youth rally and then traveled back to Nashville on their tour bus. I slept on the couch in the front lounge of the bus and gazed wide eyed out of the window at the nighttime Chicago skyline and the early morning scene on the outskirts of Nashville.

Then, incredibly, in the summer of 1998, Steve Campbell called and asked me, on Peter Furler's behalf, if I'd consider coming on the *Step Up to the Microphone* tour to do some speaking on behalf of Teen Mania and to act as a tour pastor. After a phone conversation with Ron Luce of Teen Mania, a visit to their headquarters in Texas, and a trip to Romania to see one of their mission teams in action, the plan was confirmed.

So in September 1998, I headed out for the first of two one-month-long stays on the road with Newsboys. At the age of nearly thirty-eight, when most sane people in Christian music were deciding to come off the road, I was embarking on a journey that now eight years later I still have not finished!

Life on the road with Newsboys was perhaps the most intense experience I have ever had. I learned so much about myself, about being away from my family, about life on the road, about Christian music, about relying on the Lord, and I saw so much of America—places like Memphis, Los Angeles, Las Vegas, New Orleans, which I had often seen on TV but never in real life.

I'm immensely grateful to the guys at Alliance, to Gary Smith, and to Newsboys (especially Steve Campbell, who along with his wife, Simone, looked after me so well) for the opportunities that came my way at this time. *But how does all this connect with Third Day?* I hear you ask. Good question!

The support act for Newsboys on the first part of the *Step Up to the Microphone* tour was none other than—you've guessed it—Third Day!

The first mention of Third Day in my journal, dated Saturday, October 3, 1998, reads: *"At another Paramount theme park. Third Day talked me into going on the Top Gun ride with them—a frightening experience."* I have to confess that my fear came not from being with the guys of Third Day but from a deep aversion to theme-park rides.

I spoke on the weekend shows of the tour and would be waiting in the wings of the stage while Third Day performed their set. I hadn't listened to their music before the tour but found that songs like "My Hope Is You," "Consuming Fire," and "Peace" really helped me worship the Lord and receive His strength before I went on to speak.

I met John Poitevent at this time, who became a great friend. On my first night of speaking, John was walking offstage with a guitar (he doubled as a guitar tech), and just before I was going on stage, he prayed an awesome prayer for me. I was amazed and remember thinking, "Wow! These Third Day guys must be incredible; even their guitar tech is a mighty man of God." He was actually Third Day's full-time road pastor, and it was he who encouraged me to get to know the band and to spend some time with them on our days off.

My friendship with Third Day came to fruition in October 1998. Newsboys were big into motorbikes and were going to spend some time biking in California and Nevada, so Third Day invited me onto their bus. We bonded on a golf course in Pasadena and in a Thai restaurant in Hollywood! Our friendship nearly came to a premature end a few days later when I tried to impress the crowd at a concert with my newly learned American slang, courtesy of Third Day. Great embarrassment for me and for them!

As far as my journal entries go, I joined in a Sunday devotional with Third Day for the first time the day after the Top Gun ride and led my first Bible study with the guys on Tuesday, October 13, 1998, at the invitation of John Poitevent: *"Leading a Bible study with Third Day today—supposedly. Didn't think Newsboys bus would arrive at the venue in time. Got here with twenty minutes to spare, washed and ate, only to find all the guys in Third Day still asleep."*

The first study I ever shared with Tai, Mac, Mark, David, and Brad was on this verse: "For the kingdom of God is not a matter of talk but of power" (1 Corinthians 4:20 NIV). As if to enforce that theme, the daily reading in my own quiet time from a book my wife, Gill, had given me was from Paul's second letter to the Corinthians: "But we have this treasure in jars of clay to show that this all-surpassing power is from God and not from us" (2 Corinthians 4:7 NIV).

I was homesick, missing my wife and family, aware of the grace she showed in allowing me to travel to the USA, yet I was also conscious that God was beginning to open up a new chapter of my life and that His power would be all that I needed.

I spent another two months in the spring of 1999 on the *Step Up to the Microphone* tour, although Third Day wasn't in those shows. I also traveled with Newsboys on their *Love Liberty Disco* tour, which took place inside a giant blow-up air dome in parking lots or state fairgrounds during the spring of 2000. I kept in contact with Third Day and even found time to pop into the studio in Nashville when the band was mixing the

Time album. I can vividly remember listening to the finishing touches to "Your Love, Oh Lord" and then going out for a good ol' barbecue meal together. The guys first invited me to join them for a few days out on tour towards the end of 2000. By then, John Poitevent had gone back to Atlanta to work with his church, and Third Day was touring the *Time* album. From then on, I joined them regularly on each of their tours.

The contemporary Christian music scene often receives criticism for being a business or for merely mimicking the mainstream music scene or for attempting to create a parallel and "safe" Christian culture away from the real world. And to a certain extent, all of these observations carry some truth. Yet my experience also tells me that Christian music does transform lives, does communicate with people, does help seekers find faith, and does build up the body of believers. It's for these reasons that I do what I do with Third Day.

I often reflect on what I have done to deserve the privilege of pastoring Third Day. In reality, it's down to the grace of God because there are thousands of faithful, inspirational, even famous pastors in the US who in human terms should be doing what I do. However, as I reflect, I do believe that part of the reason has been my willingness, ever since God called me to serve Him, to be faithful in the small things. I am reminded of the words of the master in the parable of the talents: "The master was full of praise. 'Well done, my good and faithful servant. You have been faithful in handling this small amount, so now I will give you many more responsibilities. Let's celebrate together!'" (Matthew 25:21 NLT).

From my late teens, when I knew God's call in my life was to share Jesus with others, I have always been excited about the opportunity to preach and teach the Word of God, whether to five hundred people or to five people. In fact, the denomination in which I grew up sent me around London to preach in many of its dwindling churches. Sometimes I would take other young people with me, and we would outnumber the small congregation we were visiting. Once I preached in a church that had space for eight hundred people, but only a handful were present. Rather than get resentful or despairing, I was always thrilled to give a message I believed the Lord had given me. Over the years I have attempted to keep that same desire to prove faithful in the small things, and I believed that opportunities such as those with Third Day would not have come my way if I hadn't treated "smaller" responsibilities faithfully. Sometimes people ask me how to become a road pastor, or they tell me that they want to be a famous preacher or a successful singer or worship leader. My advice to them is to start serving the Lord right where they are and learn from being faithful in the small opportunities that will come their way.

Through the song "Consuming Fire" God gave me much of the vision and direction for a project called Ignite, which over the last six years or so has grown to dominate the ministry I help direct in the UK. Very rarely is there a Third Day concert without the song being sung. Here Mac opens up about "Consuming Fire":

I honestly don't remember exactly how this song started out—I just remember it always being one of our songs. I have always felt this is a great representation of what Third Day is. It's a rock song, yet the lyrics are worship. It's a 6/8 song, so there is a "sing-along" feeling to it as well.

MAC

I got the idea from the verse in Hebrews. I didn't totally know what it meant when I was writing the song. I took it to mean that God purifies us in the same sense that extreme heat purifies precious metal. But we have to allow God to do that daily so it's not just a one-time shot. The song has lasted the test of time because there is an intensity in the song musically and lyrically asking God to change us and to help us. It starts from a place of brokenness and desperation. We need God to be our Purifier, our Redeemer.

"Since we are receiving a kingdom that cannot be destroyed, let us be thankful and please God by worshiping him with holy fear and awe. For our God is a consuming fire" (Hebrews 12:28–29 NLT).

Mac Powell, November 2006

2

WANNA BE A ROCK STAR

-ROCKSTAR-

I wanna be a rock star
But, I ain't got the face
I wanna be a rock star
But, I ain't got what it takes

MAC

When people listen to the song "Rockstar" once, they might not get the story behind the song. But when you get into the song, you see that it's about realizing our place in life. We may want to be famous, but God has much more in store for us. God has called us to His purpose that goes way beyond being famous or being a "star." When I was younger, I definitely wanted to be a famous singer. The desire wasn't so much to be famous, but to be heard. We see entertainers, actors, and musicians who want that fame, but we have learned what's even more fulfilling than that is to follow God's purposes.

Mac Powell, November 2006

We're all sitting in the dressing room minutes before Third Day is about to go on stage. It's San Antonio, Texas, on the *LiveWire* tour. Suddenly, someone floats the idea of starting the set with a different song than usual. The idea gets kicked around for a while, and Mark suggests the classic "Rock and Roll" by Led Zeppelin. We listen a couple of times on an iPod, people work out the chord progressions, Mac rehearses the lyrics, and it's going to happen! The crew guys—lights and sound—will be as surprised or bemused as the audience. Then we enter the land of the surreal: I make an offhand comment that the song needs some blues harmonica (I used to play a little a few years back); Geof Barkley enthusiastically agrees, and after a quick audition with Mark playing acoustic guitar, I've been recruited for a solo! Ten minutes later I'm walking off the stage to loud applause from the audience, having used Mark's microphone, shared a solo with Brad, and been introduced to the crowd by Mac. Reaching the anonymity of the backstage area, I think to myself, "Did that really just happen?" I've been on the stage a few times with the guys doing Q and As, but the San Antonio concert was my one brief episode as a rock star!

Often people will ask Third Day how they started. Mac and Mark are the best ones to tackle this for us:

I remember singing in a high school presentation when Mark came up to me afterward. We knew each other from march-ing band, but Mark said, "Hey, man, I didn't know you could sing. Why don't you come and join our garage band?" That started Mark and me playing together. A while later I quit the garage band, but Mark and I decided to form a Christian band. Then about a year later we played at a church where the youth pastor introduced us to Tai and David. Before too long, we were all involved playing together and recording demos. In fact, I'm pretty sure that one or two songs from those demos ended up on our first album. I can also remember when we signed with a small independent label called Gray Dot Records, Mark and I went down to Florida on a pro-motional tour, trying to persuade radio stations to play our record. Another strong memory is hearing Brad play guitar for the first time. He was playing in another band, and we asked him to hang out and play with us and to consider joining Third Day. "Consuming Fire" was the very first song we played as a five piece; it was a magical moment. Then there was the occasion when we were playing a small church camp and Reunion Records sent two guys along to listen to us. The president of the company said he wanted to sign us and help us with our career. That was a big, big turning point for us.

Mac Powell, November 2006

Mark Lee is acknowledged as the band historian and the man with a great memory. So here's his *detailed* account of the early days:

The first band Mac and I were in together was an unexpected one—the John McEachern High School Marching Band. He was the drum major, and I played trombone. Although we didn't know each other extremely well, we hung out at various times playing sports or going over to friends' houses. I still give him a hard time because one time we were playing football and he tackled me and tore my favorite shirt. The real story though was why a bright peach-colored shirt that said "Georgetown" on it was my favorite shirt. Another time I remember talking to him at school, and we both said that if we were ever in a band, it would be cool to do what bands like the Black Crowes were doing, as opposed to the pop metal that was dominating the airwaves at the time.

Toward the end of my senior year in high school, I began to take an interest in playing guitar. I had several friends who played instruments, and many days were spent after school practicing at someone's house, although I'm not sure what for. At first we were trying to get a "demo" together because one of the guys had a "connection" at a local club where we could play. Then we devised a more serious plan: we'd get a full band together to play for a talent show that was going on at our high school. We had no problem with guitars. Everybody and their brother could play guitar. In fact, we had so many guitars that we would ask one of the guitar guys to slide over to the bass, depending on the song. Drums were easy too. We had a guy who could play drums pretty well, and he owned his own PA. But we were having problems coming up with a vocalist. That's when I remembered Mac.

Earlier that year, I had sat in the back of the new gym and rolled my eyes during the senior assembly. I don't remember it being particularly bad, just a lot of teachers speaking and telling us about our responsibilities and how we were going to be starting college soon. I started to tune it out after a while. Then they announced that Mac Powell was going to be singing. That got my attention. I knew Mac as drum-major-Mac, the fun-loving, easygoing guy I hung out with in band. I thought about that torn Georgetown T-shirt I had at home. Then he started to sing. I think it was some Phil Collins song, but it really didn't matter what he was singing—I was blown away.

With that image in mind, I approached Mac after class one day. We had the long and involved conversation so typical of guys in high school:

ME: Dude, do you want to be in this band we're getting together for the talent show?

MAC: I can't play guitar.

ME: No, man. We want you to sing.

MAC: OK.

That was pretty much it. I wish I could say it involved a big fanfare and a light beaming down out of the sky, but I'd be lying.

The talent show never happened. But we did have a chance to play for a school function right before graduation. It was a song that Mac had written called "The Next Rainy Day," and it was pretty good. We did a few "shows," if that's what you'd call them, that summer. They were really bad. We would play at somebody's house who was having a party. We'd get together a few days before and try to learn about thirty songs. And then a couple weeks later there'd be another party, and we'd get together to learn a different batch of thirty songs. We might have been pretty good had we ever played the same songs twice. One night I was over at Mac's house, and we'd just had kind of a heated conversation with the other guys because Mac wasn't comfortable with the lyrics of the songs we were singing. After the other guys left, I asked Mac if he wanted to start a Christian band. I'm not even really sure I knew what a Christian band was. For several weeks we both had been getting serious about our faith. We had many conversations with friends about God, and Mac had even begun reading his Bible regularly. And in that moment at Mac's house, it just made sense for us to sing about these kinds of things as well.

So that was the beginning of the band. It was Mac singing, me on guitar, and our friend Billy Wilkins on keyboard. We would play wherever we could: churches, youth groups, or retreats. We weren't extremely serious about it yet—we didn't even have a name, but I think one thing that set us apart early on was that we wrote our own songs; Mac was coming into his own as a lyricist. We started out as an acoustic group, partly because we were into many of the bands that were doing the "unplugged" thing at the time, but mainly out of necessity. We didn't have a drummer or bass player. After a few months, we felt it was time to start looking. We tried a few different guys, but it never worked out. Then we did a show at my church called HollyFest. Another group, the Bullard Band, opened up, and there was a young drummer and a bass player in that band. One of the guitarists talked to us after the show and told us that he was the youth pastor of those two guys. He suggested that we give the drummer, David, a call because he had a recording rig in his basement and might help us record a demo.

Mark Lee

David's got his own slant on those important early days as well:

The very first day I met Mac and Mark, in late 1992, they came over to my house and just started showing me the songs they'd written. Immediately I thought, "Wow, there's something here that's different than any little start-up band or new songwriters." Another standout moment was the concert when the Reunion Records guys showed up. I knew they were going to sign us; I felt very early on that everything was going to work out.

David Carr

Everything certainly did work out for Third Day, and they have become one of the highest-profile and highly respected Christian bands of all time. Their albums and tours have consistently drawn plaudits and fans aplenty. Life on the road is certainly a privilege, but it isn't always the glamorous life some people expect it to be. In the summer of 2005 the band flew over to the UK for a series of concerts. I was to meet them early in the morning in the arrival lounge of Gatwick Airport in London. I began to get worried when passengers from the Atlanta flight had finished coming through the arrival gate and there was no sign of band or crew. My stress levels rose when I heard an ominous announcement over the public-address system: "Will Nigel James, meeting a party from Atlanta, please ring Immigration on the internal phone system."

After just a short conversation with the immigration official, it was apparent that Third Day didn't have the correct work permits; in fact the band didn't have any permits, and without them they weren't going to be let into the country. Tired and confused, the band had asked the official to put out a call to me in case I was in the arrival lounge and could assist. Placing the phone back in its cradle, I faced a moment of panic: Third Day was about to play a concert in the UK for the first time—on my patch, my turf—and we hadn't organized the work permits. What a disaster! I called my colleague Gary Smith, who in turn called the agency we had paid to arrange the permits. After a while he called me back; the agency had blundered big time, and the application for permits was still on a desk in their office. I endured another difficult conversation with the immigration guy, who assured me in no uncertain terms that the band wasn't coming in without permits and that, as far as he was concerned, they'd be on the next flight to Atlanta. To make matters worse, he told me that his daughter sang in the band of a prominent UK worship leader and that, personally, he'd never heard of Third Day and doubted that they were genuine!

Shortly before this, I'd written a book about "outrageous prayer" and had spent a whole tour with the guys learning how to be bolder in our prayer life. So while Gary was doing the same in Cardiff, I stood in the arrival lounge at Gatwick Airport, boldly praying that God would work a solution to allow the band to enter the UK. Only five minutes or so after my very negative conversation with the immigration official, I called him again, ready to beg him to help, when before I could even open my mouth, he said that the guys would be allowed in but that we needed to make sure we had permits arranged for a week's time when they came back into the UK from the mainland European shows! I don't think Mac, David, Tai, Brad, and Mark had ever been so pleased to see me, and I was sure relieved to see them.

A LESSON FROM THE ROAD

SUCCESS

How do we cope with success? How do we define *success*? Where do we think that success comes from?

The real problem with success is pride. Like the person who wrote the book entitled *Humility and How I Achieved It*, sometimes we are last to see it as our problem. We all are vulnerable to pride. Humility is very difficult to achieve, and the process is often painful.

How should we judge the success of a tour?

- Audience numbers?
- Units sold?
- Audience approval?
- Money made?
- Concert reviews?

None of these things are wrong in themselves.

Or we could judge the success of a tour on relationships with

- Fellow band members
- Other bands
- Crew
- Promoters
- Fans
- Wives
- God

In his book *At the Crossroads: An Insider's Look at the Past, Present, and Future of Contemporary Christian Music*, Charlie Peacock quotes Philip Yancey quoting Helmut Thielicke about Nazi Germany: "The worship of success is generally the form of idol worship the devil cultivates most assiduously."

Peacock also has much to say about worldliness:

> *The term worldliness represents thinking and doing in ways contrary to God's ways. Worldliness is connected to what the Bible refers to as the "basic principles of the world" . . . the ideas and systems of the world may have succeeded in transforming us more than we've transformed the world . . . worldliness exhibits self-centeredness.*

Fame, Fame, fatal Fame
it can play hideous tricks on the brain
but still I'd rather be Famous
than righteous or holy, any day

—Morrissey

The Pharisee in Luke 18 and Nebuchadnezzar in Daniel 4 both faced problems of success and pride. In different situations, each felt he had it made, that he was a great success. Both of them had difficulty realizing they needed to be humble.

Two men went to the Temple to pray. One was a Pharisee, and the other was a dishonest tax collector. The proud Pharisee stood by himself and prayed this prayer: "I thank you, God, that I am not a sinner like everyone else, especially like that tax collector over there! For I never cheat, I don't sin, I don't commit adultery, I fast twice a week, and I give you a tenth of my income."

But the tax collector stood at a distance and dared not even lift his eyes to heaven as he prayed. Instead, he beat his chest in sorrow, saying, "O God, be merciful to me, for I am a sinner." I tell you, this sinner, not the Pharisee, returned home justified before God. For the proud will be humbled, but the humble will be honored. —Luke 18:10–14 NLT

The Pharisee made the terrible mistake of believing he was better than other people—success often does that to people. He thought he was superior to the tax collectors, the thieves, and the adulterers of this world. He also made the elementary error of believing that God was interested in outward show rather than inward attitude. In short, he was proud of his successful position, and that got in the way of God.

Nebuchadnezzar, living six hundred years before the Pharisee, had even more reason to be proud. He was a king who ruled over many people, and that made it hard for him to submit to anyone, even to the Lord Almighty. Nebuchadnezzar's mistake was that he believed his own publicity. He took credit for his position, his power, his wealth, and his possessions. He spoke all the right words about God in public: "I want you all to know about the miraculous signs and wonders the Most High God has performed for me. How great are his signs, how powerful his wonders!" (Daniel 4:2–3 NLT). But deep down his heart was greedy, self-centered, and self-gratifying. The Lord warned Nebuchadnezzar in a dream and told him that only after a time of great suffering would he learn to truly worship the Lord and understand the Lord's greatness and his own unworthiness.

Daniel, on the other hand, had a different perspective on life and on success: "The purpose of this decree is that the whole world may understand that the Most High rules over the kingdoms of the world and gives them to anyone he chooses—even to the lowliest of humans" (Daniel 4:17 NLT). Daniel's faithful acts of private worship demonstrated that he practiced what he preached. For Nebuchadnezzar, the road to realizing that God was responsible for his success had several stopping-off points: madness, humility, faith, and recognition of the glory of the Lord Almighty.

There is a simple but painful road to humility, and according to Jesus it is a conscious choice; we have to humble ourselves: "I tell you, this sinner, not the Pharisee, returned home justified before God. For the proud will be humbled, but the humble will be honored" (Luke 18:14 NLT). We have to see ourselves in a true perspective, seeing our weaknesses as well as strengths and letting God take His rightful place. In a world where everyone tells us to look after number one, this may be tricky, but the starting point is to recognize the depth of our pride.

We all need to develop our full potential—God can make our lives both prosperous and meaningful—but we always must remember God's part, depend on Him, and offer Him due credit and thanksgiving. Of course, in the Christian music industry we face a battle to be humble because the whole system is geared toward bands and artists becoming "stars." The apostle Paul was prepared to be "the scum of the earth, the refuse of the world" so that the gospel could be preached (1 Corinthians 4:13 NIV). Then he declared, "I am crucified with Christ" (Galatians 2:20 KJV). How do you think Paul would have coped with being a Christian rock musician, given the above statements?

> *"It is one thing to follow God's way of service if you are regarded as a hero, but quite another thing if the road marked out for you by God requires becoming a doormat under other people's feet. . . . Are you ready to be sacrificed like that? Are you ready to be less than a mere drop in the bucket—to be so totally insignificant that no one remembers you even if they think of those you served? Are you willing to be poured out and exhausted?"—Oswald Chambers*

> *"If I could give you information of my life, it would be to show how a woman of very ordinary ability has been led by God in strange and unaccustomed paths to do in his service what he has done in her. And if I could tell you all, you would see how God has done all and I nothing. I have worked hard, very hard—that is all, and I have never refused God anything."—Florence Nightingale*

In an industry where we are pampered, honored, and treated as valuable commodities by executives and audiences alike, the challenge is accepting that we have no right to be treated like that at all. However hard it may be, we need to recognize that our time, our possessions, our money, our status, and even our decision making can't be of paramount importance; in fact none of these things really "belong" to us at all.

During the years of traveling with Third Day, including the harmonica-playing episode, I've had a few "rock star" moments. All of them have been simply because I've been with the band in the right place at the right time. I've found myself meeting actors, musicians, TV personalities, and sportsmen; and I've stayed in some great hotels, eaten in fine restaurants, and been driven around in a limo. For example, there was the time in LA when I found myself, along with the band, having lunch in the house of actor Thom Wilson, who played the character Biff Tannen in the *Back to the Future* films. In Atlanta I had a pass into the VIP enclosure at a U2 show, and while in Portland I had a guided tour around the Nike campus.

Perhaps the rock star thing was rubbing off on me too much in Houston on the *Wherever You Are* tour when we participated in the Gulu Walk. This was a three-mile walk around a downtown Houston park to identify with the thousands of children in Uganda who each night have to travel to a safe place to sleep. I was wearing a black Third Day cap and a pair of see-through sunglasses. Tai ribbed me about my "Bono" look, and Mac reckoned I looked more rock 'n' roll than the band. The sunglasses (very cheap, by the way) stayed in the bottom of my case for the remainder of the tour!

How Does a Road Pastor Measure Success?

It's a constant challenge for me to evaluate my role as road pastor and particularly to attempt to quantify the work I do. Just as I was leaving Atlanta at the end of the *Wherever You Are* tour, Mac came up to me and told me that even though I might not always realize it or the band might not often express it, God was using me to help them immensely. The other guys in the band actually remind me of this occasionally, but the "success" of a road pastor is a difficult thing to define.

A band member can judge his day's work on his performance in a concert, a lighting engineer by the slickness of his light show, a promoter by the number of tickets sold, a merchandiser by the per-head dollar amount spent in the evening, a local crew guy by the speed and accuracy of the load-in and load-out of equipment. But what about the road pastor?

We were in Los Angeles early in 2006; our day had been full of business and social activity. Third Day's booking agent was in town, and understandably there had been loads of business chats. A few moments before show time I paused the conversation in order to say a short prayer for the concert that evening. After I had said "amen," the booking agent jokingly laughed, "Your work is done for the day now." It was a humorous comment, but it did send me away to reflect on what else God was asking me to accomplish, besides a short prayer just before each concert started.

Here's how I define how successful I might be in the role of road pastor:

—PRAYER AND BIBLE STUDY

I strongly believe that the Lord speaks more powerfully into the lives of the band than I am able to. So I can simply be a catalyst for that to happen. Therefore I put effort into gathering the guys together regularly for Bible study and prayer times. Some of the Bible studies are reproduced in this book.

—FOCUS

During a long and arduous tour, it's not always easy to remain totally focused on the ministry God has called us to. So now and again I am able to help refocus the band on its calling and mission. Often that is an easier thing to do because I am one step removed from the intensity of being in the band itself.

—PASTORAL CARE

Being friends with all the guys in the band means that friendly conversations—sometimes with two or three, sometimes one to one— are a regular part of touring life. I've always been a good talker, but traveling with Third Day, I have learned to become a good listener! Tour manager Jenn constantly reminds me that I'm the right person in the right place at the right time because of the relationship stuff I am able to help with.

—THE CONCERT ITSELF

Our constant prayer on the road is that the Lord will use Third Day in a concert setting to minister into people's lives. Graciously, God answers that prayer night after night. Being just a small cog in that wheel and seeing the presence of God impacting people's lives remind me of the worth of my role.

I've been in many situations where Third Day, either as a band or as individuals, has been misrepresented, misunderstood, or unfairly judged. It goes with the territory, I guess, for both artists in the public eye and Christians involved in ministry. People will always be looking for you to step out of line, do or say the wrong thing, and they don't always treat you with the grace and mercy with which they would want to be treated themselves. I can remember well a group of intense young Christian adults protesting outside of a Third Day concert. They claimed that Third Day was "of the devil," and to justify their ridiculous and hurtful accusation, they stated that drums played the devil's rhythms and that the guys in Third Day didn't even have Christian haircuts or wear Christian clothes. I couldn't reason with them as to what exactly they meant by "Christian haircuts" and "Christian clothes."

It's out of circumstances such as these that the song "How Do You Know" came about:

—HOW DO YOU KNOW—

So many times I've lost my step
But never lost my way
How do you know, how do you know
When I don't know myself

Criticism can be a nasty thing. We've all been on the giving and receiving ends of it, and even for the giver it's never pretty. However, it's amazing how critical believers can be of one another at times. It's as if when we receive salvation, we are given the authority to hold everyone around us accountable to our own personal convictions and ideals. Sometimes we can give off the impression that we "know it all"!

Dealing with criticism is never easy, and the song "How Do You Know" asks the question: How do you know what I'm supposed to be doing? The tone of the chorus lyrics might give off a bit of a sharp attitude, but the real expression of the song is a simple, honest question: How *do* you know? It's not to say that the line between sin and righteousness needs to be blurred, but oftentimes there is more than one righteous or godly response or action to take. For example: Do I take this job or that job? Should we put our kids in public school or homeschool them? Should we take our music to the mainstream audience or stay where it's safe? These are just a few examples of questions we need to work out with God individually. Our job as fellow believers is to pray for one another and ask God to impart His wisdom Himself to His saints. The high horse of legalism and piousness needs to be led to the water and drowned. When that happens, the freedom of God's grace as expressed through the church will change the face of our culture.

Mac Powell, on the song "How Do You Know"

We live in a hero-worshiping generation where we would love for someone to do all our spiritual disciplines for us. Like a superstar of whom we can say, "I wish I was like him." Or a rock star we can admire from afar and believe is perfect in every way. Yet the disciples Jesus chose were a bunch of failures, doubters, ordinary people; but God used them anyway! They

simply began to look more to Jesus than to their own circumstances, making a choice to be Jesus people rather than being
defined by anything else.

3

COME TOGETHER

-COME TOGETHER-

We've got to come together
'Cause in the end
we can make it—alright
We've got to brave the weather
Through all of the storms
We've got to come together

Third Day's current road manager, Jenn, always reminds me that she believes I turn up on the road at exactly the right time, and this confirms to her that God is in control. Looking back I can see this pattern and how the Lord acts as my travel agent. I'll sit down with the touring schedule and my diary open and begin to ask God for wisdom for the upcoming tour. When will I arrive, and to which city will I fly? When will I leave the tour? What will be my route home? At which strategic concerts or events do I need to be present? What priorities in my family and ministry life in the UK must take precedence, and which will I have to miss? I'm not too popular when I've been away from family birthdays or social events! Yet it does seem that I have the habit of being on the road with Third Day at the right time.

Toward the end of the *Wherever You Are* tour, it became apparent that the guys were in a transitional stage as far as management went. They felt that they needed to change management companies, and the band had arranged meetings with a couple of prospective new companies. I managed to get to the first meeting, but although we'd tried every flight option, I missed meeting up with the second management team. However, an even bigger challenge was to unfold.

My task, should I choose to accept it—in the words of *Mission Impossible*—was to get all the guys in the band together in the same place at the same time, without distraction, for long enough to seek God's guidance and to hear the thoughts of each member so that a decision about management could be made. With time on the tour running out, and some family members out on the road with us, the task *did* feel pretty impossible. Eventually we rented a room at the back of a restaurant for a brunch together only to arrive and find they had let other customers use it. Swiftly moving to another nearby restaurant, we grabbed a table in the public area with me quietly praying that the meeting would not become loud or contentious or that a bunch of Third Day fans would not spot us. None of my fears were realized, and what was a difficult meeting to arrange actually became a meeting where consensus, enthusiasm, and a real excitement about the future quickly overcame us all. It reminded me of a few years before. . . .

It's Oklahoma City, and we're on the *Come Together and Worship* tour. For weeks the band has been discussing future vision and direction. Now we have found time to sit out in a park and spend all afternoon talking, dreaming, praying, and asking God for wisdom about the next step for Third Day. The conversations and direction of that afternoon lead to the *Wire* album, and we spend much time considering how the band could reach a wider audience and, especially, get their music heard outside the walls of the Christian community.

Many Christian bands have attempted to "go mainstream" and have done so with different motives. Often they have been misunderstood—"selling out" or "going secular," "losing their passion for Jesus," and other such phrases being leveled at them. I'm not in a position to comment on other bands, but I can very clearly remember the conversations the guys of Third Day and I had sitting on the grass that afternoon in Oklahoma City. We saw reaching outside the church and into the mainstream as a mission opportunity. It wasn't just about selling more albums or playing bigger concerts—in fact successful Christian bands that move out of the Christian-music genre often end up starting again with small album sales and low-key promotional tours or support slots to established mainstream bands.

Six of us sitting in a circle on a grassy embankment attracted some strange looks, but the topics of our conversation were important ones. How would lyrics need to adapt, if at all, for a wider audience? What would Mac, already a superbly accomplished communicator, say between songs to a wider audience? Would the guys be prepared to play support slots for mainstream artists? Did they realize that stepping outside the walls of the church meant that prayer and Bible study didn't become less important but more important? How would we explain to faithful fans the heart of the band for this new direction? How would we deal with Christians who might misunderstand what the band believed God was calling them to do? We look back to that afternoon in Oklahoma City and remember it as a crucial time when God not only spoke to us but also gave us a sense of unity of purpose and an excitement about the future that could only have been from the Holy Spirit. There was a genuine thrill about being on this journey together.

Years later, toward the end of the *Wherever You Are* tour, we were reminded about those feelings. The band was thinking about a change of management and was looking to move into a new season of ministry. Meetings and discussions in the middle of a busy tour were proving difficult, and at times tensions were running a little bit higher than normal. Yet at the right time we were able to find a few hours to meet in a restaurant and seek a unified vision. With remarkable ease and in a short space of time, there was consensus, enthusiasm, peace, and faith about the future.

Like most guys, I like hanging out with other guys, especially brothers in Christ; and some of my all-time-favorite "guy times" have been with Mac, Mark, Tai, David, Brad, and, over the years, keyboard players Geof Barkley and Scotty Wilbanks. Third Day has been together for well over twelve years, and a band doesn't survive that long unless there is a genuine feeling of friendship, even brotherhood, present. Traveling to the US a couple of times every year is easy for me because I genuinely look forward to meeting up with close friends.

Even when I was on the road with Newsboys and Third Day was the support act, I would often spend days off with Third Day. In fact, I can remember one memorable occasion in St. Louis when we all played golf together. I hadn't played for a few years, and using rented clubs I completely missed-hit a tee-shot that flew off at an angle at the speed of a bullet and hit the front of a public transport bus with a loud noise. Desperately trying to redeem the situation, I mentioned that most bad golfers couldn't hit the side of a bus, but at least I'd hit the front of a bus! In those days all the guys in Third Day hacked around on the golf course, but that's no longer the case. There have been other developments too since those earlier days, as Mac explains.

-CRY OUT TO JESUS-

When you're lonely
And it feels like the whole world
is falling on you
You just reach out
You just cry out to Jesus

MAC We have come along way since we first started, and we have been through a lot as individuals and as a band during the eleven-plus years we've been together. We have grown from young bachelors with hardly a care in the world into happily married "mature" men with many children and responsibilities. The one thing I have grown to realize is that not only do I have burdens and responsibilities, but also I am able to see and understand that others have the same burdens and trials. When you are younger, you know that burdens are there, but you can't fully understand their impact until you are older. As a band, we have had many friends and family members who have experienced significant hardships and loss over the past couple of years, so a song like "Cry Out to Jesus" was a natural extension of what we have been going through. In each verse of the song, there are specific people in my mind—each line I sing is directly connected with someone I know. My hope is that you are also able to connect personally with each verse through your own experiences. Not only do we all know these people, but also we are these people. In those times of trial, I hope we can remember that we can find our strength, peace, and hope when we cry out to Jesus.

Mac Powell, talking about the song "Cry Out to Jesus"

Of course, the friendship and bond between the guys in Third Day started long before I came on the scene, and these friendships have lasted the test of time. When the guys are at home in Atlanta, they quite rightly devote time to their wives and children, but out on the road they enjoy each other's company. Let me take you through a typical day in the life of a touring band—but we'll start our tour after the concert.

Once the band leaves the stage—to high fives and congratulations all around—they'll head back to the dressing room. This is a special time, made even more special by the after-show food that Jenn, the road manager, has ordered. In between consuming mouthfuls of food, taking showers, packing suitcases, and handing in-ear monitors back to the road crew, the guys review the show and listen to each other share how they feel the concert went. Most often this time is a reflection on a job well done, with some observations for minor adjustments on the coming nights. Occasionally friends and well-wishers will pop their heads around the door, but normally this is band-only time: I'm privileged to be a part of this, not least because I get to share in the food!

Pretty soon conversation turns to what we'll do once we get back onto the tour bus: it might be watching a DVD of tonight's show or a music DVD one of the guys has recently purchased; sometimes it might be catching up on a must-see TV series, and often the guys will introduce me to their latest favorite movie (being from the UK, I always get to see the latest releases late!). Now and then one or two of the guys will want a more involved conversation about something, so they'll either stay in the dressing room as late as possible or head out to the bus quickly.

When the crew members who travel with the band have finished their responsibilities and the bus driver, Champ, has arrived from his rest in a hotel, the bus is ready to roll, and we drive off into the night onto the next venue. Unless the movie is really gripping, people begin to drift off to their bunks or perhaps to watch something else in the rear lounge of the bus. I could spend this whole chapter just listing great late-night bus memories with Third Day, but tonight I'm off early to my bunk. I'll see you in the morning.

The guys get up at varying times on the morning of a concert. Some will be up very early to do radio interviews; one or two of us might head off to the golf course with Brad, or if it's summer, Mac and Mark will make sure we visit a baseball stadium.

The crew guys will have been working hard all day in preparation for tonight's show, and sometimes the band itself will have a sound check in the middle of the afternoon. Generally we'll gather back together around the time of the evening meal. After we've eaten, we'll make time and space for a devotion, and we'll pray for the concert that night. The members of Third Day are always concerned that the concert won't be "just another show," but that each night will be unique. The devotional time gives us an opportunity to pray for each other as well.

Oftentimes Tai slips out because he'll be speaking on stage on behalf of World Vision or Invisible Children. Back in the dressing room, he puts on his cowboy hat; Mac does some vocal warm-ups; David makes us all laugh with his fantastic impersonations of characters from movies we've been watching; and final choices for stage clothes are made. We join hands for one final prayer, and then there is a knock at the door. One of the tour management people is ready to escort the guys to the side of the stage, and tonight's show is only minutes away.

I'll either watch the concert near the monitor engineer at the side of the stage or from the farthest seat possible. Way up in the back of the balcony is a good place to get an overview of the sound and lighting and to keep an eye on how the crowd is enjoying the show.

One of the most significant times we've had together in our devotions was when we looked at the theme of "Outrageous Prayer." Back in Cardiff, Wales, my friend Carl Brettle had introduced me to the concept, which God then used powerfully among Third Day during one tour.

A LESSON FROM THE ROAD

OUTRAGEOUS PRAYER

Outrageous prayer is simply praying in faith to the Lord and expecting to see Him answer.

It springs from the biblical reality that when believers combine together in prayer they bring God's power to bear and they can be assured of Christ's presence:

I also tell you this: If two of you agree down here on earth concerning anything you ask, my Father in heaven will do it for you. For where two or three gather together because they are mine, I am there among them. —Matthew 18:19–20 NLT

If we really believe these verses, then we can use this agreement in prayer very powerfully. Jesus uses the Greek words *pantos pragma-*

tos, which literally translated means "every practical matter." To bring God's power to bear, we need to agree. Jesus uses the word *symphoneo*, which means to "sound together." This reminds us that the Holy Spirit loves to work in unity and that for there to be action in heaven there needs to be unity here on earth.

Do you remember the story of the paralyzed man who was brought to Jesus by his friends? He was bedridden and certainly couldn't have made it to Jesus on his own, but he had a bunch of friends who really cared for him, and they made sure that he reached Jesus:

> And the Lord's healing power was strongly with Jesus. Some men came carrying a paralyzed man on a sleeping mat. They tried to push through the crowd to Jesus, but they couldn't reach him. So they went up to the roof, took off some tiles, and lowered the sick man down into the crowd, still on his mat, right in front of Jesus. Seeing their faith, Jesus said to the man, "Son, your sins are forgiven."—Luke 5:17–20 NLT

It was the faith of his friends that enabled Jesus to forgive the sins of the man, and even more:

> Then Jesus turned to the paralyzed man and said, "Stand up, take your mat, and go on home, because you are healed!" And immediately, as everyone watched, the man jumped to his feet, picked up his mat, and went home praising God. Everyone was gripped with great wonder and awe. And they praised God, saying over and over again, "We have seen amazing things today." —Luke 5:24–26 NLT

It might be that we feel paralyzed about a specific concern or worry in our lives. We might lack faith for something we have almost given up praying for, in which case our friends can carry us to Jesus and pray on our behalf. We need to stand in agreement with each other and pray for breakthrough. We'll "pray outrageously" for each other and believe that God will answer.

After that, over the next month or so on the road, we met together to pray outrageously. One by one, each band member shared intensely personal concerns he desperately needed prayer for. Using the image of the paralyzed man and the power of agreeing in prayer, we lifted each one to the Lord in prayer. These times together were incredibly powerful. We shared stuff we'd never spoken about before; there were tears, there were genuine concern and love for each other, and there was willingness to bring the power of God to bear into situations and circumstances that individually each of us had either given up praying about or never had the faith to pray about in the first place. Family stuff, band stuff, future plans, friends who were hurting, personal walks with the Lord, and relationship concerns were just some of the areas we each asked the rest of the guys to pray outrageously for. Over the weeks of these devotions, we learned at a deep level what it means to pray for each other and to intercede on each other's behalf. How is it that Third Day has survived as a band for so long? David gives us his view:

A constant subject that comes up in interviews is the unity of Third Day and how we keep it strong. It's no easier to answer than it is to implement. Unity depends upon a lot of factors for any union of souls—be it a marriage between man and woman or the pseudo-marriage of the members of a band.

DAVID

We've all been through a lot together on the road: home sickness, disagreements over various issues such as the general direction of the show, and just plain weariness from being in a different and unfamiliar place each day. There is also something to be said for times of depression that each of us can go through from time to time. More than any of that, we have each experienced so many personal changes through the years as we've aged and grown up. We were kids when Third Day started. Now we're all married and we have a small army of kids ourselves. And that changes everything.

Through it all, though, a sort of unspoken common goal of Third Day has been to simply celebrate this incredible gift we've been given. We are indeed grateful for the success we've enjoyed—as are our families. There have been times where it felt like the only thing holding us together was the success. That doesn't sound great to say but I just believe it is one of the things the world uses for selfish gain but something that God has used to keep us moving along. And at the end of the day there has always been this comforting resolve that we are not in as much control of our destiny as we think. We are mere instruments in a larger orchestra with a better conductor. That is something to rally around as a band and to find unity in!

Now it might sound good to say that we are all so deeply close to one another and just the best of friends but it would be less than truthful. And besides, is that really the goal or the purpose in life? I *do* believe any one of us would give our right arm for another if it came to it, so that makes our friendships much deeper than we may even realize at times. There is no doubt that everyone who represents Third Day, be it band members, wives, or kids are much more woven together than it feels to us at times and God has made his stamp on our lives very visible. We are busy people and our on the road/off the road lifestyles open the door for much opportunity to be distracted by the less important matters of life which can often squelch unity, so we count it a blessing to have the lasting friendships that God has given us in each other.

David Carr, November 2006

So here's my analysis of the five guys in Third Day. Five guys, each of whom I am extremely proud to call friend. To ensure that there is no favoritism, I'll describe them in alphabetical order.

Tai Anderson:

Not necessarily the best bass player in the world, but the best-*looking* bass player in the world. Tai is simply one of the people I most enjoy being around. When Jesus talked about bringing life in all its fullness, He could have been using Tai Anderson as an example. He's all energy and has more innovative thoughts and plans before breakfast than most of us do in a week! This was never more graphically illustrated than on our tour of Australia in January 2007. We were in Brisbane and due to fly out in the morning to Sydney. I had a single room in the hotel, but the guys were sharing; David and Tai were paired up.

David wanted to fly out very early the next morning to catch up with friends in Sydney and asked me if I'd mind swapping rooms and sharing with Tai. Of course, I said yes but didn't really know what I was letting myself in for. I went to bed first and was dozing, watching some rugby on TV. Tai came in around 1:30 in the morning and proceeded to ask loads of questions about rugby, started debriefing about the tour so far, reviewed booking procedures for overseas tours, and then talked about some family stuff. After a while I was falling asleep, so I excused myself, turned off the TV, and put my head down. The next thing I knew, I heard the shower on and assumed I'd overslept and jumped up in a panic. The time was only 5:30 in the morning, and Tai was already up. I dozed off again to be woken at 7:30 by Tai brandishing sheets of paper. He'd already been to the hotel's business center and written out a series of propositions as a result of our conversation a few hours earlier. That's Tai—passionate and committed to the ministry of Third Day, forever pursuing excellence and, to use a British phrase, "mad as a badger." Tai is not ashamed to put his arm around male friends, and I've appreciated that affirmation from him on numerous occasions. He vies with David as king of the one-liners and has a sense of humor that either makes me giggle uncontrollably or hang my head in despair! Tai's growing assurance as a public speaker has done much to engage Third Day fans with important issues of justice and compassion overseas, and he practices what he preaches.

Brad Avery:

He's my golfing buddy! A man of constant encouragement to me on the golf course, Brad is a perfectionist where his own game is concerned. Graciously he takes a hacker like me out on golf courses all over America, and I enjoy his company immensely.

Brad's desire for perfection spills over into his music, and he can often be seen at sound check making detailed changes to his onstage equipment. Brad and I are closest together in age, although I'm still a good few years older, and that means some of our musical heritage overlaps. We had great fun together one night on the tour bus watching a documentary about heavy metal music. We could remember many of the bands mentioned. Brad is always the first one up when we are on the road, and his morning routine faithfully includes stretches and exercises along with a healthy amount of time in the Word of God. Brad is a deep thinker, and even with his music and his golf, he always desires a deeper walk with the Lord.

He's very much his own man but, like the other guys in the band, willingly takes responsibility for his own spiritual journey and always has a Christian book in his bag to stimulate his thinking.

In 2010, golf's Ryder Cup tournament is to be held in Wales, and I'd love to think Brad and I could be walking the fairways cheering on the US and European teams respectively.

David Carr:

The two of us really shouldn't be compatible because David is a car connoisseur and a skillful man as far as home improvements go. I, on the other hand, am definitely not either of those things. Furthermore, he's a consummate drummer, and I'm a wannabe drummer (put it this way, my drumming is worse than my golf!).

Yet whenever we talk about faith, life, and family, David and I find that we have so much in common. David is desperate to cut through Christian cliché and find reality. He's scrupulously honest about his own shortcomings, and he often vocalizes what the rest of us are really thinking but too afraid to say. For example, David will articulate that his biggest "ministry" challenges aren't as a member of a high-profile rock band but as a husband and a father.

Brokenness, humility, and desperation for God are some of the marks of a disciple that David carries with him. I can well remember the time at a concert venue when David engaged a security guard in conversation throughout the day and then led him to Christ after the concert. He's right up there with Tai as far as humor goes, has a great ability to mimic people, and can remember all the funny lines from our favorite films and repeat them in the right accent. He's also a lover of certain British comedians, although his attempt at the accent sounds like a character out of *Mary Poppins*. Along with Tai, David is also a regular visitor to a certain chain of coffee shops, so we'll often have good talking times together over a cup of coffee. For me, David is best summed up by Acts 13:22: God said David "is a man after my own heart."

Mark Lee:

How best to describe Mark Lee? A fine guitarist, a rock music expert, an avid reader, a prolific blogger, and a big fan of college football; those will do for a start. For many years Mark and Mac have had a pact that whenever they are in a city that has a baseball stadium, they must try to visit it, if they possibly can. I've gate-crashed that pact over recent years and have enjoyed many great days at the ball game. Mark is a real encouragement to me because often on his own blog or on the Third Day site he will make reference to a devotion I've shared, and it's always a relief to know that someone was actually listening. Mark once took me along to a conference in Nashville themed around Bob Briner's book *Roaring Lambs*. The conference was full of believers from Nashville, New York, and Hollywood and focused on influencing culture. Mark was in his element and was well respected among the plethora of writers, producers, artists, theologians, and academics.

Mark's most endearing quality is that he totally gets my

quirky, British sense of humor and will often catch a joke or funny saying that others miss completely. Everybody loves someone who laughs at his jokes! Mark also has a very southern drawl, and I can listen to him talk for ages. The America I dreamed about as a kid and I saw on TV comes alive in conversations with Mark Lee.

Mac Powell:

Mac is the most recognizable member of the band—after all he is the front man, and his voice and looks are very distinct. His passion for baseball has rubbed off on me, and I've attempted to educate him and Mark about cricket. An immensely respected figure in the Christian music industry, Mac nevertheless needs plenty of verbal affirmation. I guess because he knows the impact of verbal affirmation for himself, Mac is great at giving it to others. Whenever I arrive on tour and whenever I leave, Mac always makes a point of telling me that my presence is valuable to the band—and specifically helpful for him. Actually, through Mac and Tai, much of my British reserve has been broken down, and I'm no longer embarrassed to tell a brother in Christ that I love him. Mac is another disciplined reader and will often come to me with a theological question arising out of a book.

Mac's often the movie-trip organizer as well, and I regularly arrive back home having seen all the top movies before they've even been released in the UK, thanks to Mac. Along with Tai, David, and Mark, Mac has opened up his home to me on numerous occasions, and for that I'll always be thankful. Like Mark, Mac embodies for me all that I'd imagined a good ole southern boy to be, and I've learned not to get between him and a TV set when Alabama is playing football.

When I see Mac singing on stage or speaking between songs or leading thousands in worshiping the Lord, I'm aware what a gifted front man he is. Many of us would love to be as accomplished as he is in just one of these areas, yet Mac is always aware that these gifts come from God, and he endeavors to be a wise steward and a conscientious leader.

4

PUT YOUR HAND IN MINE

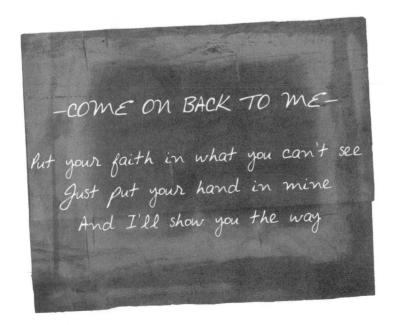

—COME ON BACK TO ME—

Put your faith in what you can't see
Just put your hand in mine
And I'll show you the way

E aster 2005, the *Wherever You Are* tour rolls into Nashville. It is going to be a busy time because besides the concert and a gold disc presentation there is a two-day Gomer Gathering of Third Day's most hard-core fans. I've been asked to lead devotions for the Gomer Gathering at the start of each day. On the second morning the worship band will be none other than Third Day themselves playing acoustic versions of some of their most loved worship songs, but for the first morning, worship will be led by the guys in Hyper Static Union.

Meeting the band face to face and hanging out with them for a short time is an incredibly exciting time for Third Day fans. The guys spend considerable time on the road talking to fans, signing autographs, walking around meet-and-greet rooms, and posing for photos. After so many years doing this kind of thing, it can become stale and at times even tedious. For the band it's just another day, but for fans it could be one of *the* days of their lives. This was brought clearly into perspective to us when we all went to see U2 play in Atlanta. I'd already seen U2 in my hometown of Cardiff, Wales, but Tai generously offered me a spare ticket for the Atlanta show. I spent most of the evening next to Mark Lee and Third Day's production manager, Dave, in the VIP area in front of the soundboard. The rest of the guys and their wives were up in seats, and Tai tells the real story:

I know whenever anyone talks about Bono, a debate among Christians is sure to follow: You know, he used to be a Christian. Is he still a Christian? How can he be and drop the F-bomb on the Golden Globes? Well, he is doing a lot for Africa, but didn't you read that article where he got drunk and passed out on the floor of some bar in New Orleans after the Super Bowl? What's with that headband anyway?

Bono has become one of American Christians' favorite topics. I think my church is going to have a Sunday school class just to debate Bono's faith next year. So, writing this entry, I know I'll stir up a few comments and criticism. But I've got a pretty decent story to tell that I've managed to wrangle into a bit of personal revelation, or is that relevation? Never mind, that was last tour.

You see, U2 has always been my favorite band. My sister bought me *Unforgettable Fire* when I was about nine, and I've been hooked ever since. Growing up, I had posters on my wall, U2 guitar songbooks, T-shirts, you name it. U2 is a big reason I ended up in Third Day. They've always blended spirituality with great rock music. So to me it was the most natural thing in the world. Since I grew up on U2, I never understood why rock music was always associated with rebellion. To me, it has always been about soaring melodies that wake you up, make you think, and stir your soul. When I was hooking up with David, Mac, and Mark in the early days of Third Day, I didn't really understand what all comes with being in a "Christian" band. God seemed like the only topic worthy of a really good power chord.

My tastes diversified in high school. REM and the Black Crowes were local legends. Pearl Jam and Nirvana were on the scene. Anyone in a rock band has to learn to play some Led Zeppelin. But at the core of it all was always U2.

A few years ago Mark and I had the opportunity to meet Bono when he came to Nashville to enlist CCM (Contemporary Christian Music) artists in DATA's (Debt, Aid, Trade for Africa) efforts to end extreme poverty in Africa. Mark and I had been to South Africa a few months before with Habitat for Humanity, and we were very keen to hear what Bono had to say. A lot of awesome things came from that meeting.

A bunch of artists did a tribute album to raise funds, and Jars of Clay started an amazing foundation called the BloodWater Mission to bring fresh, clean water to Africa. Brad, Mark, and I made a trip to Lesotho in southern Africa to experience firsthand what AIDS is doing to Africa. Since then, we've tried to direct as much attention as possible to World Vision's HOPE child initiative, which specifically targets children in regions hardest hit by AIDS.

CCM artists and fans really grabbed on to Bono's mission. I know a lot of the political results of DATA's efforts came about because American politicians finally realized how many of us are concerned about the AIDS crisis. It's been amazing to be a part of a sort of revival among believers where we've realized that our faith shouldn't just compel us to improved behavior but also toward a sense of mission and justice for the world.

Anyway, sorry for preaching. A few weeks ago we had the opportunity to see U2 at Philips Arena in Atlanta. The folks at DATA hooked us up with passes so we could go backstage and talk with Bono before the show. Since I knew this was coming, I immersed myself in U2 fan geekdom for a solid week. I listened to all my records, I watched DVDs, and I even read a new book entitled *Bono: In Conversation* where Bono pretty much lays out his life story, faith, and philosophy. During the time I was reading the book, we were out on the road doing the *All Access* tour. Every night after the show, we'd sit at an autograph table for over an hour signing CDs and talking to fans. I was living out both sides of the fan experience. I was receiving it every night after the concerts with countless stories of inspiration and appreciation. But I was also experiencing the other side of fandom as I was getting prepared for the U2 show and our meeting with Bono. All week I was questioning what it means to be a fan. It is short for fanatic, you know. What do fans really want? What did I really want from Bono? As I was reading the book, one part really spoke to me. Bono talked about meeting Bishop Tutu and asking him for a blessing. He went on to say that he has always craved the blessings of older men he respected. Everyone from Bob Dylan, Willie Nelson, and Johnny Cash to the pope and Billy Graham had given Bono what amounts to a blessing. Bono talked about how Jacob tricked Esau to get the blessing from Isaac. Why didn't God intervene? Maybe because Jacob valued the blessing more.

Well, the light bulb turned on. What do fans want? Fans want a blessing. Fans want to be appreciated; they want to be acknowledged; they want to be lifted up. I turned to Mac in the front lounge of the bus and told him that I now knew what I wanted from Bono. I wanted a blessing. I wanted my hero to validate me. Lofty, I know. But musicians are supposed to dream big.

The night of the show we headed to the concert. I was the point man with the tickets, so I got to experience the other stressful part of being a fan—picking up tickets at will-call, parking, meeting up with the group, and passing out the right tickets and passes, etc. We finally got it all sorted out and headed to the meet-and-greet area. In there were probably about fifty people. Basically, Bono was going to walk in on his way to the stage. We were all spread out having conversations when Bono walked in talking to the head of the Centers for Disease Control and Prevention, located in Atlanta. He took a picture with a girl having her fourteenth birthday. Then he turned to us. The conversation was brief: he basically thanked us for our help and asked us about our trip to Africa. We snapped a picture and he was gone. We didn't have a chance to chat it up. He didn't invite us on the plane to finish the tour with them or open any shows. He didn't tell us that *Conspiracy No. 5* was still his favorite even though it has sold the least. He didn't ask us why we don't play "Thief" or what "Blackbird" was about. We met, and we went to our seats.

Then the concert started, and it was probably my least enjoyable concert experience ever. This was not the band's fault; it was because four people walked into our aisle completely wasted, stumbling and cussing and screaming. They told David's wife to move and were getting in our face. David asked to see the guy's ticket, and he took out a dollar bill instead. Finally one of the guys took out his ticket—which had them seated way at the other end of the aisle. But they stayed right in front of us, yelling and cussing. After David got an usher, they slid over to their seats. Now I was standing right next to the loud, extremely drunk man. U2 was doing its fourth song, and the guy was screaming in my ear twice as loud as Bono was singing from the stage. My blood started boiling. Every thirty seconds, the guy would bump into my shoulder. Bono was talking in between songs, and the man was screaming expletives at the stage. My veins started popping. I took off my jacket and handed it to my wife and asked her if she had bail money. She pleaded with me not to do anything; "You'll get kicked out." I started not to care; I couldn't hear the concert anyway. As the band began playing "Love and Peace, or Else," he bumped me again. By this time, I had a whole kung fu scenario acted out in my head. I clenched my fists. Then he knocked me over into my wife, which knocked her to the ground. I stood up and grabbed the man by the neck, and I guess you could say that I instructed, no, *commanded* him to change places with his girlfriend. I vented, and . . . he moved. Five minutes later he was gone, probably in a cab heading home.

There was "controversial" Bono on the stage singing about love and peace while "Christian" Tai was tearing into the guy and thinking about how to elude police in the event of an unintended homicide. Did I feel justified? Absolutely! Did I feel righteous? Absolutely not! When I get really worked up, it takes me a while to calm down. The band started playing "Pride in the Name of Love," exalting the nonviolent methods of

Martin Luther King and Jesus, and I had just spent the last twenty minutes thinking about extracting my justified vengeance on the drunk next to me. I felt sick to my stomach. As they started "Where the Streets Have No Name," I prayed: *God, forgive me for losing my temper; thank You for helping me to not totally lose control; help me to calm down and relax. Amen.* Well, "Streets" is a great song to get you thinking outside of yourself. I was loosening up and finally began to enjoy the concert. Then it happened. After "Where the Streets Have No Name," Bono started talking about how great it was to be in Georgia. How a lot of great music has come from Georgia. REM is an incredible band. Third Day is here tonight. . . . I didn't hear anything else. I stood there with my mouth open. My wife looked at me with her mouth open. Did Bono from U2, the biggest band in the world, just mention Third Day in the same sentence as REM? As Bono talked about Africa, and the band started to play "ONE," tears streaked down my cheeks. Bono asked us to get out our cell phones and text our names to UNITE, an SMS (short message service) code, to sign up for the ONE Campaign. Since I had signed up a year earlier, I took the opportunity to text Mac with this sentence: "We got our blessing."

Tai **Anderson**, November 29, 2005

So often I had talked with the band about relating to fans. On the thirty-eighth night of a tour, after a draining ninety-minute set, sometimes the last thing you want to do is sign autographs, enter into a conversation, or have your photo taken. For the band member it can be just another night, but for the fan who's waited two years to see her favorite band of all time play live, this is one of the most significant moments of her life. A smile, a few positive words, a CD cover signed, or a photo willingly posed for becomes a blessing that carries a massive impact. On the night of the U2 show in Atlanta, the band realized for themselves just how powerful that is.

A LESSON FROM THE ROAD

The Three Friendships Everyone Needs

As we talk about authority and accountability issues and the responsibility to encourage an emerging generation of younger Christians, we recognize the need for these three types of people in our lives:

- A Paul
- A Timothy
- A Barnabas

AN OLDER EXAMPLE AND A YOUNGER PERSON TO ENCOURAGE

The apostle Paul committed himself to help the younger Timothy grow in his faith. In modern-day words we would say he discipled or mentored Timothy. In his final days in a Roman prison cell, Paul chose to write to Timothy with some final words of encouragement and advice. He reminded him that they had a friendship and a relationship that was like father and son:

> You then, my son, be strong in the grace that is in Christ Jesus. And the things you have heard me say in the presence of many witnesses entrust to reliable men who will also be qualified to teach others.—2 Timothy 2:1–2 NIV

When Timothy read this letter, he would have remembered loads of shared experiences together: mission trips, miraculous conversions, preaching, arrests, and plenty of signs of God at work. This long-lasting relationship was based on three things:

—A RELATIONSHIP BASED ON A POSITIVE CHOICE

> He came to Derbe and then to Lystra, where a disciple named Timothy lived, whose mother was a Jewess and a believer, but whose father was a Greek. The brothers at Lystra and Iconium spoke well of him. Paul wanted to take him along on the journey, so he circumcised him because of the Jews who lived in that area, for they all knew that his father was a Greek. As they traveled from town to town, they delivered the decisions reached by the apostles and elders in Jerusalem for the people to obey. So the churches were strengthened in the faith and grew daily in numbers.—Acts 16:1–5 NIV

It would have been easier for Paul to go it alone, but he wanted to take Timothy, to invest in him, and to help him grow in ministry and maturity. It was a tough choice for Timothy to decide to travel with Paul. He had to get circumcised so that his status as a Greek wouldn't offend the Jews he would be meeting. In effect, Timothy had to turn away from his own background and culture in order to learn from Paul. The result, however, was that the early church grew daily in numbers.

—A RELATIONSHIP ESTABLISHED OVER TIME

> I thank God, whom I serve, as my forefathers did, with a clear
> conscience, as night and day I constantly remember you in my
> prayers. . . . For this reason I remind you to fan into flame the
> gift of God, which is in you through the laying on of my hands.
> —2 Timothy 1:3, 6 NIV

Paul laid hands on Timothy right at the start of their time together;
and now, years later, he was still urging Timothy to use the gift God
had given him. Timothy, by this time, was probably a grown man in his
late thirties or early forties, and Paul is still desperate to see Timothy's
destiny in God fulfilled.

I've found a modern example of this type of relationship. Jamie
Oliver, "the Naked Chef," is a popular TV personality. In the project
called "Jamie's Kitchen," he took twelve disadvantaged young people
and determined to teach them all he knew about cooking and then set
them up for life as chefs. By the end of the project, he had mortgaged
his house to pay for the restaurant they were working in; he'd spent
hours and hours each day with them, excited about their successes
and upset with their failures; he'd given second and third chances and
had been let down and lied to; and he'd given master classes in the
finest cooking skills. And, eventually, he had come out with a handful of
top-quality chefs. Jamie Oliver had invested a year of his time, money,
energy, enthusiasm, and knowledge into these young people.

Of course, this modern-day example lacks one crucial thing Paul and
Timothy had:

—A RELATIONSHIP FOCUSED ON JESUS

> So you must never be ashamed to tell others about our Lord. And
> don't be ashamed of me, either, even though I'm in prison for

Christ. With the strength God gives you, be ready to suffer with me for the proclamation of the Good News.

It is God who saved us and chose us to live a holy life. He did this not because we deserved it, but because that was his plan long before the world began—to show his love and kindness to us through Christ Jesus.—2 Timothy 1:8–9 NLT

In the first chapter of Paul's second letter to Timothy, we see the name of Jesus mentioned eight times in eighteen verses, and God the Father is mentioned eight times for good measure. So it's not just about following an older leader. It's about following a man or woman who is focused on God:

—A GOOD FRIEND

Think about what I am saying. The Lord will give you understanding in all these things.—2 Timothy 2:7 NLT

And you should follow my example, just as I follow Christ's.
—1 Corinthians 11:1 NLT

In the early days after his conversion, Paul was fortunate to have Barnabas vouch for him with the disciples. They were naturally suspicious of Paul, because he'd been a persecutor of Christians, but it was Barnabas who made sure that Paul was welcomed and accepted:

Then Barnabas brought him to the apostles and told them how Saul had seen the Lord on the way to Damascus. Barnabas also told them what the Lord had said to Saul and how he boldly preached in the name of Jesus in Damascus.—Acts 9:27 NLT

Barnabas was just the type of reliable and honest friend everyone needs:

> Barnabas was a good man, full of the Holy Spirit and strong in
> faith. And large numbers of people were brought to the Lord.
> —Acts 11:24 NLT

Here are some questions to discuss:
- Do you have a Paul figure in your life? An older, more experienced Christian to help you grow.
- Do you have a Timothy figure in your life? A younger, less experienced Christian you can help grow.

Remember that you are never too old to need a Paul and never too young to be a Timothy.

- And what about a Barnabas? A reliable friend who will be with you and be honest with you. Sharing the good times and the bad.

Being respected veterans of Christian music, the guys in Third Day recognize that they are able now to have a mentoring role with younger, less experienced artists and have gone to great lengths to offer opening slots to up-and-coming performers. Mac, in particular, is passionate about the role he can fulfill with younger artists.

I've always had a desire to find artists who have potential and help them develop. We've been given such a great platform, and one way to use it is to help other artists develop their craft, to make better music, and to get them heard by a wider audience. It's something I spend a lot of my time away from

Third Day doing, but collectively we've all had a hand in Hyper Static Union, for example. In the early years of Third Day, we weren't helped so much musically, but there were plenty of people who gave us advice and wisdom to whom we owe a debt.

When you are looking for a younger musician to help develop, you definitely want to look for someone who has talent! Personally, I'm also looking for someone who can sing and who can write songs, has a great heart and is spiritually at a place where he or she has something to share, and has the drive to do what it takes to make the whole thing work. I love producing, but it's more about helping an up-and-coming artist with his or her craft than just producing a record. I bring to the table the experience I have in writing and arranging songs, and I want to help someone make the best three- or four-minute song he or she possibly can. One of my favorite studio sayings is, "Trim the fat." Sometimes people like to over-elaborate with lyrics or length of the song, and I aim to cut things away that don't need to be there because they aren't helping the song.

With Hyper Static Union, we spent time helping them look at their stage performance—what was the best order of songs, what approach they should take as an opening band. We've been there and done that, so we shared our experiences.

Mac Powell, November 2006

David is another band member who finds time to get to know newer artists and spend time in discussion with them.

When a younger band comes to us for advice about becoming successful, I reply with what is often seen as a cliché but is true and very important: build a fan base. Of course, then they ask, "How do we do that?" and that's the sixty-four thousand dollar question! The answer has to be to make music people want to listen to and want to become fans of. It's important not to forget what attracts you to songs you like and what makes you become a fan of a band. Oftentimes it's that catchy song you keep on singing to yourself. We have been fortunate that since the start of Third Day that we've had fans who genuinely like our music and believe that it speaks to them at a heart level. Even in those early days it wasn't just our friends patting us on the back and saying, "Well done"; there was always a growing number of fans. I don't know how to reproduce that for someone else, but the relationship with our fans has always been vital to the success of Third Day. There's perhaps a few hundred of them we know quite well, hundreds more who have shaken our hands or to whom we have given an autograph, but there are thousands and thousands more we'll probably never meet. Perhaps many of them will read this book!

I think about our fans a lot, especially around concert time when I see five thousand or so of them in the audience. We'll recognize a few faces from our fan club, the Gomers, in the front row; but there are other people out there who come to Third Day shows, listen to our CDs in their cars, or play our songs to their friends. It's bizarre to me when I think about it, but it's the music that connects them to us. I've noticed that extreme fans of sports or music often find their identity in the sports team or the band they are fans of. They wear all the merchandise, check out all the websites, and almost become obsessed. We call those fans "hard-core," and I have to admit that sometimes we can be unsettled by that approach.

I've been there myself and have thought about my identity as "the smooth coffee drinker" or "the guy who drives cool German cars." It sounds silly when I articulate it like that, but each of us wants to find identity somewhere. Although we appreciate and are flattered by the devotion of the hard-core fans, we hope that they'll find their true identity in Christ, not just in being a Third Day fan. I'm aware that many people, including me, get tempted to make an idol out of someone or something and inadvertently replace God. We don't want anyone to worship Third Day! Part of our daily challenge as members of Third Day is to live out of our identity in Christ, because if we have been born again, then that's where our real identity lies.

David Carr, November 2006

David Carr also sheds some light on Third Day's fan club, Gomers.

With any band that's been around more than a few years and enjoyed any level of touring success and song appeal, there is bound to be the formation of some sort of "fan club." From the beginning we had talked about making an official attempt at forming a fan club for Third Day. There was the short-lived Third Herd that all twenty-six members proudly backed with multiple visits to our monthly shows at the Strand Theatre in Marietta, Georgia. Membership came with a complimentary business-card-sized identification certificate and the privilege of knowing they were in the elite circle of all things Third Day. It didn't last, and looking back it seems evident that sometimes the best fan clubs usually form on their own. Gomer was a woman from the Book of Hosea. She was a prostitute, and and yet God told Hosea to marry her and to love her despite her sin. Our song "Gomer's Theme" off our second album, *Conspiracy No. 5,* is an anthem to compare the parallel universe we live in as followers of Christ to the world of Hosea and Gomer. We are all like Gomer in our sinful state. We all cheat on God the Father and sell ourselves to the world in exchange for cheap thrills, yet God still loves us unconditionally, and with reckless abandon He pursues our hearts endlessly even while we repeat the offenses.

In 2001 a group of our sincerest fans formed the Gomers and thus changed the landscape of our fan base (and the color of the front row at most of our concerts!). Donned in bright orange T-shirts, at least a few Gomers flock to nearly every show we perform, even concerts on other continents. But one thing that makes it all make sense is the growing camaraderie among the Gomers that seems to transcend Third Day. At that point it becomes about the body of Christ, not just a band. It's just cool!

David Carr, November 2007

Third Day's fans are incredible! The hard-core Gomer fan club members are among the most dedicated and passionate fans you could wish to meet. Wherever we tour in the world, there will always be a contingent of Gomers in the audience. Over the years I have met many, many fans, and some faces become very familiar. The band might be touring the West Coast, and we'll spot a bunch of the same fans at every show—that's some commitment in terms of time, travel, and money. We might be playing a series of shows in the UK, and not only will European Gomers show up, but some Gomers from the US will have scheduled vacations or business trips in order to catch a Third Day concert overseas. When circumstances permit, a walk along the line outside a venue to chat with fans, often accompanying Mac or Tai or David, gives me an opportunity to touch base with these grass-roots supporters of Third Day's ministry. Similarly, when the guys have a signing session, either at the end of a concert or in a bookstore, I'll often walk around to meet and share the enthusiasm with fans who are waiting for that important autograph or photograph. Oftentimes, fans of the band will e-mail me with a question or a comment about some of the audio devotions I post on the Third Day website, and over the years I have taken pleasure in responding to these e-mails and to developing friendship with some of these fans.

I must admit there have been conversations between the guys in the band and me when we've wondered if the passion and involvement of the fans sometimes gets too intense and a little out of balance. It's to that end that I've spent some time putting together a how-to on being a Third Day fan.

Why listening to Third Day's music can help you on the journey.

Ever since my teenage years I have been convinced that Christian music is a superb vehicle for evangelism and discipleship and acts as a strong gateway into a deeper understanding of Scripture and a stronger relationship with the Lord. I believe that these things are beautifully demonstrated in the music and the ministry of Third Day. If fans approach the band's songs with a readiness to hear from God, then He will surely speak into their open hearts. Our greatest thrill on the road is to hear stories of God putting lives back together, turning people from darkness to light, giving hope in tough situations, mending broken marriages, directing young people to their purposes in life, and using Third Day's songs to help in these processes. It's not difficult to imagine a thirty-something married couple at a Third Day concert with their two early teen children and their own parents along with next-door neighbors who don't yet have a relationship with Jesus. All of them will at some time or another during the concert have an encounter with God.

Mac Powell loves to base song lyrics directly on Scripture, and these songs can help unpack biblical truth and give us spiritual insights that otherwise we might not have picked up.

I make a habit of using Third Day songs in my own personal devotions, and often these "quiet times" turn into "loud times." Many people find, whether in the live setting or on a CD, that Third Day helps them engage in worshiping God. Remember that my very first experience of the band was worshiping through its music from the side of the stage while waiting to go on and preach.

What should a fan's expectations be concerning the heart of the band?

Fans have every right to expect that members of the band will be trying faithfully to serve the Lord as husbands, fathers, brothers in Christ, and band members and that they will be dependent on God for their source and their strength. Fans should expect the guys to be living lives of integrity, honesty, and accountability.

Fans should expect that the band will put heart and soul into album projects and that the project will be creative, entertaining, a good value for the money, and, above all, have a message worth communicating.

However, fans become unrealistic when they have an expectation that band members will be spiritual superheroes who never experience difficulty or brokenness and who always have an easy answer to every challenging situation. Each guy in Third Day faces exactly the same daily struggles as each of us—plus some additional ones most of us never experience. Fans should expect the band members to take seriously God's call on their lives together as a band and to use their public profile wisely as Christian leaders.

What should the expectations be from the guys in the band about the heart of the fan?

In some ways it would be accurate to say that band members should expect nothing from fans. By this I mean that no band has a divine right to have fans at all, that no artist has a contract that states his or her fans will buy every album produced. And the guys in Third Day certainly do not take their fans for granted.

Of course, every artist desires fans who are faithful, who spend their hard-earned cash on each new release and each concert ticket, and who champion the cause of the artist to other music fans. Third Day has given fans a "voice" on their website; and I, for one, appreciate feedback but do get disappointed when it becomes overly critical and too personal (not about me but about guys in the band). The guys of Third Day would rather their fans be "supporters" than just "consumers." They hope fans would be people who let the music minister to them, who enjoy meeting the band when the opportunity arises, who don't intrude too much into the band's personal life or personal space, and who, above all, see through the band and recognize Jesus.

How can we be partners in the gospel? What is the link between band and fan?

I like to see this partnership work on two levels. First, on a personal level: as if each band member echoed the words of the apostle Paul when he said, "And you should follow my example, just as I follow Christ's" (1 Corinthians 11:1 NLT).

In other words, don't try to be like a guy in Third Day; try to be like the Lord of the guy in Third Day. Someone once said that Christians should look like sheep from the front and like shepherds from behind. To everyone who sees the guys in Third Day as great shepherds to follow, remember that really they are just sheep following the Good Shepherd.

Second, the partnership works because Third Day is able to introduce and advocate many and varied ministries and to encourage fans to engage with and support these ministries. When Tai steps onto the stage and challenges the audience to find out about Invisible Children, for example, he brings a trust and integrity that mean this is not simply some commercial tie-in but that the members of the band really believe in this project themselves.

Here's Tai's appreciation of Third Day fans:

The relationship between band and fans is one that is always full of contradictions. On one hand, the band uses its collective brand, imaging, and marketing powers to try to convert the general populace to fan status. At this point, the fan is invited to join the band in concert, for the right price, for a night the band hopes will be full of meaning and significance. Once the fan has bought his or her ticket, it then seems as if great efforts are made to ensure that the fan has as little access to the band as possible. Armed security guards are often placed to keep the fans far from the band's dressing rooms and buses. A general secret service atmosphere seems to ensure privacy during the entire day of the show. A good portion of our media efforts seem to be focused on convincing the public and specifically current or prospective fans that we are normal people just like them. Then, on show day, great effort is made to create an atmosphere that indirectly communicates to fans that we are, in fact, not like them, that our time is more precious, and that our presence is something that only a select few can enjoy.

This process has always left us feeling quite uncomfortable, but our lives on the road exist squarely in the middle of these contradictions. We are just five guys who want to be approachable, but we're also five guys who value our privacy. We enjoy spending time with fans and friends we have met along the journey. But, at the same time, our fans' enthusiasm often leaves us uncomfortable. Despite these paradoxes, it would be safe to say that Third Day as a whole enjoys a very meaningful relationship with our fans. We are very conscious of our fans all through-out the creative process, and we are well aware that our livelihoods exist as a direct result of their support. Throughout the years I have met some fans who have shared with me incredible stories of hope and en-couragement. So often fans express the reason they like the band is that they feel we are very approachable. I think the reason for this is, and will remain the case, that we are in fact Third Day fans ourselves. When we are creating music, we rarely delve to the realm of artistic self-indul-gence. Our focus tends to gravitate toward the musical moments and lyrical messaging that will most succinctly have impact for our fans. As we put shows together, from production blueprints to nightly set lists, our focus is again on creating moments that will make lasting memories and meaning in our fans' lives. As Third Day fans ourselves, this process is much easier than it seems. We don't live in an artistic nirvana, oblivious to the songs and musical moments to which our fans relate. We tend to like the same songs our fans like. There is a reason that the hits are hits, and we enjoy playing them because the real fun is when the audience is participating with as much enthusiasm as we are.

We've felt for ourselves the power that a Third Day show can have. We experience ourselves the moments that keep fans coming back, and we stay hungry for more. We recognize the collective band as something bigger than our individual selves, and we desire for the band to be at its best each night. Ultimately if we have a bad night or aren't cutting it on any given song, we know it in the same way the audience knows it. What gives us a real connection with the fans is that they know we know it, but they also push us on to be at our best. So, when those moments happen—when the concert is really a concert and when the music bridges the gap in just the right way—the fans and the band are all in it together.

Tai Anderson, October 2006

5

SING A SONG

-SING A SONG-

I want to sing a song for You, Lord
Lord, for You I want to sing a song
And I want to lift my voice to Heaven
And listen to the angels sing along

I can remember vividly the first time I listened to Third Day's songs. It was in early September 1998, just before heading out to the US to go on tour with Newsboys. Discovering that Third Day was going to be the support band, I rummaged through a pile of CDs I'd been given earlier in the year at the GMA conference in Nashville. Sure enough, *Conspiracy No. 5* was one of the free CDs I hadn't gotten around listening to. I thought to myself that if I was going to be meeting these guys soon, I should at least catch up on their music. I enjoyed the album but didn't realize that some of the songs on it, and more, would become very significant in my life before too long.

Third Day's ministry is an intricate mix of original songs, well-produced albums, and relentless touring. What at times might simply appear to be the act of singing a song takes on so much more significance in the lives of legions of fans— whether listening to a CD or watching the band live. What about the band members themselves? What did the songs mean to them when they wrote them or now when they play them? Does the same song in the same spot in the concert night after night retain the same impact? How do the guys approach each concert afresh? Does each concert leave a powerful memory? Is it possible? Well, let's discover.

DAVID

I try to offer my drumming to God as worship, especially if I'm having a tough show. I'll be thinking about something completely different—organizing my CDs at home—and I have to consciously move back to worship. I tried raising my hands in worship once in a concert, but it didn't really work; the timing of the song went to pieces!

Funny, but the songs that excite me the most, we have never ever played live! "Give" from *Time* would be in the set list if it were up to me. I love the lyrics and the mood from the song "I Don't Know" from *Come Together*, and "Blind" from *Wire* would also feature on my fantasy set list. Those are the types of songs I really enjoy. Of the stuff we play in our set, "Tunnel," "Come on Back to Me," and "Creed" are the songs I enjoy playing live. About "Creed": I was a big fan of Rich Mullins, and as a kid I used to go to a church where we said the creed every week, so it's a very special song for that reason. All of us in the band have our favorite songs, and each member of the audience does, too. I'd really have a blast with my own personal set list, but it might be kind of boring for everyone else!

David Carr, November 2006

I'm sitting in a Starbucks just outside of Atlanta; Tai Anderson's truck is parked outside, and it's full of Third Day suitcases. We've just come back overnight on the tour bus from a run of four concerts in Florida on the *Wherever You Are* tour, and the guys are doing some breakfast radio before they head back to their homes. Champ, our bus driver, has headed off now, so I'm looking after luggage until the guys finish the radio stuff. On the way to unload bags, Champ and I were having a conversation about miles traveled with the band. I reckoned my 200,000-plus miles of transatlantic flights was pretty impressive until Champ matter-of-factly mentioned that over the years he had driven well in excess of 750,000 miles for the band. That puts into perspective the sheer volume of concerts and the longevity of Third Day's career so far.

This chapter reveals that a commitment to hard work, travel, and a strong vision are some of the prerequisites for a lasting and fruitful ministry. In other words, we are going to delve

into some of our memorable tours and concerts.
Tai takes us back to the early days:

TAI

One of my most memorable concert moments is quite an unlikely choice. When I think back through the years, we've had some amazing shows. At times we've played for tens of thousands at festivals around the country. We've packed out clubs in London. We've played in rock clubs and arenas. The audience has often been so loud that we couldn't hear ourselves onstage. However, one of my most memorable moments came quite early on in the band's history. It was probably about 1996. We had just played at a church in Tulsa called Guts where they have a cutting-edge outreach to the unchurched, bikers, and street kids. After the show, the audience gave us a "love offering" for payment. That gave us gas money to make it to our next show, a *Disciple Now* weekend at a Baptist church in Longview, Texas. We were going to be the band for the weekend, doing a couple of concerts and leading worship for the one hundred or so high school students.

On the way to the show, I picked up a hitchhiker on the side of the highway. Growing up I had always heard stories of how people had picked up hitchhikers and had amazing conversations with them, eventually leading them to the Lord. To say that I was spiritually zealous at nineteen would probably be an understatement. So I picked up this guy who happened to say that he was going to the same town we were: Providence. Picking up a hitchhiker is a noble, though illegal, undertaking when you're driving yourself somewhere, but when you're driving a van and trailer with other people, it's probably best to discuss it with your bandmates. By the time we made the trip to Longview, the rest of the band was pretty ticked at me for picking up a guy who had told a series of ridiculous stories for five solid hours. Who could have known that this guy on the highway was a former British secret agent who was an expert marksman and viper killer turned test pilot and, finally, a long-haul truck driver with a broken-down rig?

When we arrived in Longview, our hitchhiker headed for the non-existent Texas hills, and we headed to the church to set up for the weekend. There we found one of those situations that happened so often in the early days: the equipment we needed wasn't there. In those days, David, Brad, and I were the only ones who knew which side of a microphone to plug the cable into (which is still pretty much true). So we had the task of setting up the stage. Since I was also in charge of the merchandise, I had to set up our table in the hallway of the youth room as well.

I got into a really bad mood: the other guys in the band were ticked at me for the hitchhiker incident; a bunch of the T-shirts I had shipped to the show hadn't shown up; the PA and lights were totally lame; and to top it off, the turnout for the retreat weekend was going to be smaller than expected. In the world of a fledgling Christian rocker, this was just a really bad day.

About this time, I took a moment to myself to pray. Whenever I read about someone praying, I imagine that person to be a great spiritual giant with a broadband pipeline directly into the throne room of God. I believe that God hears our prayers. But, I assure you, I wasn't feeling or acting like a spiritual giant at the time; I was just a ticked-off teenager who was feeling sorry for himself and not really feeling satisfied with the pace of progress my band was experiencing.

In this youth room in Texas, I had an experience where I felt, and still believe, I heard from God. Whenever anyone talks about hearing from God, a picture of a Christian giant quickly erodes to a picture of a nut job who belongs in a loony bin with a straitjacket or of a televangelist who needs just a few more million dollars. It's one thing to talk to God;

it's quite another to hear from God. However, I, and probably you, do believe that God still speaks. The question is: How do you know when it's Him talking and not just your own imagination? I've heard many a pastor describe the way to discern God's voice is that it is a voice that sounds a lot like your own but contains wisdom you do not possess. At nineteen years old, any thought containing wisdom was probably God's voice, because I assure you that I didn't contain any myself.

In that moment, I heard, felt, or thought an idea that has proved to contain wisdom I know I didn't possess at the time. The message was simple: *If you're not happy and content now, you'll never be happy or content.* That was exactly what I needed to hear in that particular moment in my life: I was getting to play music, getting to travel on the road, getting paid to play music, and I was a part of events where the gospel was going forth. What more did I want? Sexier numbers?

I hope you're not disappointed. I didn't promise a great revelation. But that simple statement has been one of the more fundamental points of inspiration and blessing for my entire life. You see, in this business and probably in yours as well and in life itself, we're always striving for the next big thing. When you're in a band, you are always looking for a higher chart position, more albums sold, or better attendance. You set goals and strive to see those goals realized. The problem is that there is often an emptiness that accompanies actually achieving those goals. After you have a number one single, anything else is a disappointment. After you sell out a theater, you want to sell out an arena. After you get a gold record, you want a platinum record. After you reach platinum, you want to double down. All that is fine and good; it's just the way life is and always will be. The problem is that so often we are never happy or content, not ever, no matter what.

We've had a lot of success in Third Day. We've achieved so many goals, and we continue to set new ones. I'm incredibly driven. I'm always looking ahead. But, foundationally for me, when it's show time, when the album sales reports are all in, I go back to Longview, Texas. Because of that experience, I've been able to enjoy the journey. So many other musicians I've met have missed it. They're never happy. Maybe it's a required ingredient to be a tortured soul—a requirement to be a truly inspired artist. But for me, I remember Longview. After ten years of incredible successes and incredible failures, I can honestly say that I've truly enjoyed it all. I've enjoyed the crowds of fifty, and I've enjoyed the crowds of fifty thousand. We've done over a thousand concerts, but the one I think about the most was a *Disciple Now* weekend in Longview, Texas.

Tai Anderson, October 2006

I've got many, many personal memories of concerts and life on the road. I'll highlight just a few here. Being part of the first-ever Third Day show in the UK in June 2004 was a real thrill for me, especially when at one stage earlier in the day it looked like the band wasn't going to be allowed in the country (I've told that story in chapter 2). While praying with the band in a cramped dressing room in the Forum, a legendary London rock 'n' roll venue, I have to admit that I shed a tear and was momentarily overcome by the emotion of the moment. Having traveled extensively with Third Day all over America, it was significant for me when they actually walked onto a stage in my home country. The band, too, rated that night as a special one—a crowd of over two thousand (massive for UK Christian concerts) knew all the words of the songs and gave the guys a rapturous reception. As well as being the MC and speaker for the night, I also spent half the concert in the local supermarket stocking up with food for the tour bus—they needed someone with local knowledge.

e, it's the seemingly small and mundane memories
n my mind as much as the *big* occasions. Similarly,
when the band performed in my home city of Cardiff, Wales,
in June 2005, it was a very special night. The venue was a
small club at Cardiff University, but it was packed out. In 2005
and 2007, Third Day played this venue—probably the smallest
place they ever play nowadays. Yet because it was my home,
and my ministry Ignite was partnering with Third Day, the
concerts took on great significance. Certainly for my friends,
family, and ministry colleagues, these Cardiff concerts were
an opportunity to see a Third Day concert and to gain a better
understanding of why I spend time with the band and the type
of ministry we offer, all over the world. Standing at the back
in the Third Day set at the first Cardiff concert alongside my
colleague Gary Smith, we reminisced about the first concert we
had promoted in Cardiff in 1995. It had been with a duo called
Phil and John, good friends of ours. Three days before the concert, we had not sold one ticket and had to cancel. Gary and I
spent the evening of the canceled concert standing outside the
church venue to apologize to anyone who turned up!

Two concerts in Sydney, Australia, at the Hillsong Conven-
tion Centre also remain in my memory, especially as each of
them was on Australia Day, which is their equivalent of Inde-
pendence Day. Being a big cricket fan as a child, I had listened
to cricket matches from Australia on my transistor radio tucked
up in bed in a cold British winter. Years and years later, I've
been privileged to visit Australia twice with Third Day and,
because of God's grace, have seen some of the cricket grounds
I had grown up dreaming about! Much more important than
cricket, though, has been the opportunity to partner with the

body of Christ across the world and meet some fine Christians. Through Third Day's tours in Australia, I've struck up a friendship with a man named Andy Gourley, who hosted us twice in the city of Brisbane. Like me, Andy is a sports fan, and he'll be coming over to Cardiff, Wales, for the next Rugby World Cup tournament to share in some sport-based outreach programs with me.

Of all the great American cities I have visited with Third Day—New York, Atlanta, Los Angeles, Chicago, Dallas, Nashville, San Francisco, Boston, Las Vegas, Orlando, the list could go on and on—one of my favorite memories is of a concert in Fort Wayne, Indiana. Fort Wayne is my home away from home because I have a close friendship with Heartland Church there, and often on days off from touring I would fly to Fort Wayne to minister in the church. In the fall of 2006 we played in Fort Wayne, and for me it was a little like two worlds colliding. Friends who I'd always try to see in between Third Day shows were now at a concert for themselves. Students who I had last seen on a spring break mission trip to the UK the previous March were rushing up to me in the lobby with greetings. A young woman who had interned with Ignite in Cardiff a few years before came along with her fiancé. For years, Mac had been gently joking with me about my frequent visits to Fort Wayne, so it was good to finally go there with the band.

Looking back over the last six or seven years, I believe one of the most important concert memories was in Belfast on Third Day's first UK tour. I had been traveling with the band for up to ten weeks a year; and through all that my wife, Gill, had faithfully looked after our children, run our home, worked full-time as a teacher, and released me to travel with the guys.

At long last, at the Belfast concert Gill would see the band perform live for the first time and meet the guys face to face. One or two of the band members had often spoken to Gill by phone and expressed their gratitude, but in Belfast, Mac made a special point of mentioning Gill and me from the stage.

When Gill saw the show and saw thousands of people worshiping the Lord and being thoroughly blessed by the music, she realized that the time I spent with Third Day was worth it. Sitting in the hotel after the concert, chatting and relaxing with the guys, Gill was able to get to know them a little and understand even more about the heart of Third Day. David Carr is my wife's favorite, but don't let the other guys in on that secret.

Third Day combined with Michael W. Smith and Max Lucado for the *Come Together and Worship* tour, and we would listen every night to Max speaking from stage about the first mention of worship in the Bible. It was in the story of God asking Abraham to sacrifice his son on the altar. Max used to explain that if we had no other example of worship in the whole of Scripture, then this one would be enough. The boy Isaac was the biggest thing that had happened to Abraham and his wife Sarah, and God was testing Abraham to see if he was prepared to offer his "biggest thing."

Over recent years Christians might have often thought worship to be a song style, but actually it's a lifestyle. Max reminded us that worshiping God doesn't mean just giving Him a few verses of a song or a Bible verse or a couple of hours of our time, but it means giving Him our "biggest thing." Worship involves sacrifice, and the theme of worship has often appeared in our devotional times. Abraham was prepared to sacrifice his biggest thing, but the rich young ruler who wouldn't give up his wealth wanted to keep his biggest thing for himself.

A LESSON FROM THE ROAD

AN AUDIENCE OF ONE

We can learn so much about worship from the story of Mary and Martha in the gospels of Luke and John.

As Jesus and the disciples continued on their way to Jerusalem, they came to a village where a woman named Martha welcomed them into her home. Her sister, Mary, sat at the Lord's feet, listening to what he taught. But Martha was worrying over the big dinner she was preparing. She came to Jesus and said, "Lord, doesn't it seem unfair to you that my sister just sits here while I do all the work? Tell her to come and help me."

But the Lord said to her, "My dear Martha, you are so upset over all these details! There is really only one thing worth being concerned about. Mary has discovered it—and I won't take it away from her."—Luke 10:38–42 NLT

Martha showed hospitality and compassion. She wanted to get the details right so that Jesus would be welcomed on His visit. What she did was good, but it wasn't the most important thing to be concerned about. Mary, however, had her priorities correct and realized that Jesus was the real worship leader, that worship is all about being preoccupied with the Lord Himself, and that true worship focuses on an audience of one—God. Even when we'd rather do something else, we need to worship—that's where the sacrifice comes in!

What we call worship in contemporary settings the Bible really defines as praise. There are three Hebrew words that might accurately describe our modern-day praise and worship: *halal*, making a noise; *zamar*, singing or playing music; and *zada*, bodily actions or gestures. However, we would do well to digest Paul's plea: "Therefore, I urge you, brothers, in view of God's mercy, to offer your bodies as living sacrifices, holy and pleasing to God—this is your spiritual act of worship" (Romans 12:1 NIV). Worship is about life, not just lips. Our instruments don't actually lead the worship—they just lead *to* the worship.

In John 11, Mary and Martha give us another contrast in attitudes. Their brother Lazarus has died, and they speak the same words to Jesus. "Martha said to Jesus, 'Lord, if you had been here, my brother would not have died. But even now I know that God will give you whatever you ask'" (John 11:21–22 NLT). Mary, however, speaks from a position of worship at the feet of Jesus. "When Mary arrived and saw Jesus, she fell down at his feet and said, 'Lord, if you had been here, my brother would not have died'" (John 11:32 NLT). It is after the words of Mary that Jesus acts and raises Lazarus from the dead. In the middle of all the despair and pain, Mary worships.

God loves our attention and delights when we want to give Him our worship. Whenever the people of God give, then He turns up, especially when we offer heartfelt praise and worship—even more so when we do it sacrificially, when we count the cost, when it's hard to worship, but we do so anyway. The Bible talks about the *shekinah* glory of God—the immediate, intense, holy presence of God. That's when our spirits get ignited by God's holy fire, and then anything could happen!

On the fall leg of the *Wherever You Are* tour, I shared these two verses from Revelation with the band:

> I, John, your brother and companion in the suffering and kingdom and patient endurance that are ours in Jesus, was on the island of Patmos because of the word of God and the testimony of Jesus. On the Lord's Day I was in the Spirit, and I heard behind me a loud voice like a trumpet."—Revelation 1:9–10 NIV

We studied the key phrase "I was in the Spirit," which in the New Living Translation reads, "I was worshiping in the Spirit." John was in exile on the island of Patmos, which was essentially a Roman penal colony. His circumstances were not good, and all around him he would have seen reminders that he was in captivity.

Yet he was able to go beyond his situation and his circumstances and could worship in the Spirit. The lesson we learned from this was that if John could be "in the Spirit," then by definition he could also be "out of the Spirit" or "not in the Spirit." We made an honest appraisal of ourselves and recognized there are times when we aren't in the Spirit, even acknowledging that it's possible (but not desirable) to pray, preach, minister, and even worship and sing from the flesh rather than from the Spirit.

In our prayer time directly after this study, you would have found us pleading with God for us to be in the Spirit and to be led by Him rather than by human instinct or direction. During the concert that evening, Mac saw a group of women together in the audience and sensed that they had story to tell. He called one of them up to the stage and gave her the microphone—a very risky and unusual strategy. The woman explained that she had been praying for an opportunity to say something. She went on to describe how her husband and child had been tragically killed in a house explosion a year or so before but that she and one other child had been rescued. For the past several months the *Wherever You Are* album had been a real comfort to her. She was at the concert with a group of friends who had been a great support for her. As she was sharing this poignant story, the crowd fell silent, and most of us, band included, had tears in our eyes. Afterward we recognized that the whole episode was an "in the Spirit" moment, and we thanked God for it.

As well as the very powerful spiritual element of Third Day concerts, the band has been a powerful influence in other areas. The guys have constantly looked for new and innovative ways of touring and have headed in directions both geographically and commercially that others haven't walked. Third Day's concert tours have often been industry leaders, not least in the area of sponsorship. When the band first partnered with a commercial company, the news attracted coverage in national newspapers and on TV chat shows. The move wasn't without criticism from within the Christian community. Mac explains:

Our sponsorship with Chevrolet was pioneering, but it wasn't always well received or spoken about positively. We believed it helped to add legitimacy to our ministry in the wider world outside the Christian community. As believers we always want to do things for the glory of God, but we also want to reach people outside the church.

The Chevy sponsorship allows us to have a better show and a cheaper ticket price so that fans get a better concert all round! Chevrolet, for its part, has been able to showcase its product to our fans and has done so discreetly. They have never told us what we can and cannot say; they have allowed us to be who we are and do what we do. I'm all for the relationship with Chevy!

Mac Powell, November 2006

One of my all-time-favorite movies is *Groundhog Day* with Bill Murray, where he relives the same day over and over again. Life on the road can sometimes feel like that unless you make some effort.

You find yourself with a great deal of time to fill, and it's no wonder that one-time keyboard player Geof Barkley and I managed to watch a whole season of *24* on DVD over a period of just four days. If you asked me in which cities we did that, and on which one of the tours, my memory banks don't hold that information any longer. Venues, cities, concerts, even whole tours, sometimes blend into each other after a while. It's not surprising that toward the end of a tour, the final question Mac will ask before he strides onto the stage is, "What city are we in tonight?"

I've described a typical day in the life of a touring band in a previous chapter, but here's David's view of a day on the road:

The interesting thing about being on the road for a group like Third Day is that every day is almost completely different from the one before. The characters remain the same; but the scenery, the food, the Internet connection, and the water pressure in the shower change (if there is a shower). Don't feel bad for us though; there is still the tour bus, the satellite television, and Fruit Loops to make us feel at home, wherever we are.

Today, we are in Ames, Iowa. We don't often make it to Iowa, and what a shame that is, because every time we do come this way, we're greeted with good old midwestern hospitality and warmth that we're used to in the Deep South. I believe the building that we're in today, the Stephens Auditorium at Iowa State University, is one of the only places we've ever played in Iowa. So while I haven't got much to go on as far as a real impression of Iowa goes, I still nonetheless have fond memories of playing here. Not sure what else the day will bring: a movie, the mall, an electronics store, or a bookstore? Or maybe we'll just chill a little and enjoy each other's company. We are now seven shows into the tour, tonight being number eight. Time really flies when you are going from place to place and having a blast playing rock shows to enthusiastic fans. I'm just amazed and humbled that after all these years we still have fans who are into what we do. It's the biggest compliment in the world! Though some of the venues we've been playing are a bit different from what we're used to, we still go out and make the best of it since the fans don't really care too much about how cool the room is or how many people are there. We know that you paid for your ticket just like everybody else and that you deserve the same show we give to an audience of seven thousand in an ultraplush arena. Spiritually speaking, we are in a really cool place these days. I feel like God is stirring our hearts a little more these days, and the message of "Cry Out to Jesus" is becoming more real to us individually. Trust us, even with sold-out shows, adoring fans, and our great jobs in general, we still have a lot to "cry out" for.

David Carr, *Wherever We Are* tour, February 26, 2006

On Third Day's weblog, Mark Lee will most times post the set list after a concert, and these days rarely are two concert set lists exactly the same. I've taken the liberty here of heading off into fantasy land and choosing my own Third Day set list. To my knowledge they have never played this set list, nor are they likely to, but it gives you an idea of my favorite Third Day songs.

A rock block to start:

> "I Got a Feeling"
> "'Til the Day I Die"
> "Did You Mean It?"
> "Get On"
> "Took My Place"
> "Sweet Home Alabama"

Then some acoustic stuff:

> "Sing a Song"
> "Still Listening"
> "These Thousand Hills"
> "You Are Mine"

Into a rock worship section:

> "My Hope Is You"
> "Carry My Cross"
> "Consuming Fire"

Back into some more rock 'n' roll to finish the set:

"I Can Feel It"

"What Good"

"Come Together"

The encore:

"Creed"

"Cry Out to Jesus"

"God of Wonders"

Now that's what I call a concert! Of course, by the time you read this, I might have some new favorites, and my set list will have changed!

THERE IS
HOPE FOR THE HELPLESS

—CRY OUT TO JESUS—

There is hope for the helpless
Rest for the weary
Love for the broken heart
There is grace and forgiveness
Mercy and healing
He'll meet you wherever you are
Cry out to Jesus
Cry out to Jesus

BRAD

Everyone gets a tiny taste of love sometime in his or her life that serves as a picture of what it could be: energizing, purifying, and freeing. Suddenly, in one fatal moment, life happens, and fragments of hope and love scatter. Scrambling to protect ourselves, we construct fortresses to shelter our battered hearts. What was built to keep us safe eventually becomes our prison. When we realize our need to escape, we find ourselves institutionalized and unable to engage. That's when love busts through the walls and sets us free.

Brad Avery on the song "Love Heals Your Heart"

— LOVE HEALS YOUR HEART —

When you think your life is shattered
And there's no way to be fixed again
Love heals your heart
At a time you least expected
You're alive like you have never been
Love heals your heart

I've been to so many Third Day concerts over the years, in so many different towns and cities, that sometimes it's difficult to remember exactly what happened when; and days, concerts, even whole tours get blurred and confused. Every so often though, something so significant happens that helps to imprint a particular day or venue on my memory banks forever.

That is the case when I look back to a concert at Willow Creek Community Church, just outside Chicago, on the spring leg of the *Wherever You Are* tour in 2006. The occasion was Willow Creeks' youth leader's conference, and Third Day's concert was going to close the event.

The previous couple of months had been difficult ones for me. At Christmas time my wife had become very ill and was not able to work until Easter time. To make things more complicated, at Christmas we had paid a sum of money as deposit on three acres of land in southern India where we were going to build a school. My wife, Gill, is a teacher and was excited about a vision that our Indian pastor friend had. His name was Prasad, and his vision was to open up a school in one of the villages he ministered in. I had visited with Prasad the previous year and had identified the land to be bought. Gill agreed to head up the fundraising project for the school, and we used some of our savings for the deposit. The agreement with the landowner was that we would pay the remainder of the cost by Easter time. That was my dilemma. I'd agreed to travel with the band for ten days or so in February and another three weeks in March, but could I leave my wife alone? And who was going to spearhead the fundraising for the land while she was ill? Would we lose our deposit and the land? Could I let the band down and not tour? In the end our eldest daughter, Rachel, agreed to move back home for a week to give Gill some company, and our youngest daughter, Bethan, came with me to the USA. She stayed with friends in Fort Wayne and managed to see Third Day once in Indiana at the start of her trip and again at Willow Creek before we flew home the next day.

Third Day has a practice of giving a percentage of ticket sales at each concert to good causes. We were early enough in the tour that these good causes hadn't been identified for every concert on the tour. We were sitting outside Willow Creek Church on the tour bus, and the conversation got around to the projects that could be supported. Now the pressure of the fundraising, or non-fundraising as it was, for the Indian school was really getting to me, and I'd been praying about it constantly. Have you heard the saying, "If you know how to worry, then you know how to meditate"? Well, I'm not too sure which one I was doing, but I was concerned. I wanted to ask the guys if they'd get involved with the Indian school project, but before I could do that, one of them said, "Hey, Nige, we should help you out with whatever you're doing in India!" Everyone quickly agreed, and before too long we had identified five concerts on the tour where a small percentage of ticket sales would go to help buy three acres of land in a small Indian village. I was thrilled, shed a tear, and cried out my thanks to God.

Gill was equally pleased when I got home and explained the situation to her. Over the next few weeks, the money raised by the Third Day concerts came in, and we transferred it over to the school account in India. It covered the balance of money needed to buy the land almost to the exact penny!

The following September I headed out to India again with a team of people. We were part of the official opening ceremony and foundation-stone laying in the village of Undeswaparum in the state of Andhra Pradesh in southern India. To honor Third Day, we had called the land the Come Together Compound, and the vision now stretches past a school to an orphanage as well. I've shown plenty of photos and films of the project to the band, but my hope is that some day members of the band will visit Undeswaparum and see the Come Together Compound in real life.

Each guy in Third Day has overseas-mission experience for himself and can articulate what it means to offer spiritual and practical hope to people. Here are David's thoughts:

When I went to Guatemala in 1995, we'd been a band for two years or so. Three weeks in Guatemala and Honduras opened my eyes to a different situation and made me realize that we can be very insular in the USA. There are so many reasons not to leave America because we have it all, but that trip opened up my soul to the fact that there are other cultures in this world and that many of them are hurting and experiencing poverty and hardships. I tried to bring back more of a global perspective to the band. Everyone was appreciative, but it's difficult to understand that stuff unless you've really experienced it. That short mission trip gave me more of a mission mindedness about Third Day. Now everyone in the band has experienced overseas mission in some shape or form.

To be honest, my mission perspective has faded in and out over the years; and while I'm excited to see Tai so passionate about Africa, for example, I need to go on a mission trip again myself to rekindle that perspective in my own life. I've seen all the films and heard all the statistics, but when you go and experience a situation for yourself, it connects with your heart. Having said that, we can use our profile as a band and our concert platform to raise awareness of countries and peoples in real need and encourage our fans to help. If we think Third Day can solve *all* the world's problems, then we've already lost; but we can bring practical, financial, and spiritual help into the places we believe that God has placed on our hearts.

I've also begun to realize true poverty is something that reaches into the innermost part of the human experience. It is not solely a lack of stuff, necessities, or luxuries, but something far more intense. There are many people who have nothing yet seem to have a relationship with the Father that I can only dream of, while many of us in western society have so much yet are so impoverished in our souls. That is a debatable and lengthy discussion we can have together, but for now we in Third Day want to reach out to our audiences and offer a glimmer of hope wherever they are. Many times I feel like saying I have everything I could ever want—health, wealth, family, friends, you name it—yet I still feel empty and lonely inside. I sometimes feel guilty for feeling this way, but I recognize that apart from Christ, nothing else can fill me and give me true identity and purpose, so I'm prompted to cry out to Jesus. I hope that you will recognize the truth that Jesus is the one who gives you your name, your purpose, and your sense of self-worth—three things that are essential to the life of a believer. Going through the religious motions won't get you anywhere if you don't start with brokenness and willingness to cry out.

David Carr, November 2006

David is so right when he articulates the same thing that Jesus talked about: the poor in spirit are not just those who are materially impoverished. Having traveled to many places of material poverty, I can honestly say it is in the western cultures such as the US and the UK where I see people who are most spiritually poor. Conversely, I can remember standing in a remote Indian village, about to speak in a small church in a leprosy colony. The whole congregation was made up of severe leprosy sufferers; their bodies were disfigured, they were experiencing physical pain, and they lived in the poorest of circumstances. I swallowed hard and wondered deep down if my preaching would make any difference to these unfortunate folk. My friend Pastor Prasad encouraged me to share that as Christians our bodies aren't a permanent residence and that our spirits will be with God for eternity. I spoke a few words, then we worshiped together. I have never experienced such an intense time of worship with people whose circumstances could have made them very angry with God. Instead, they raised their deformed arms, lifted their broken faces heavenward, and celebrated God's love for them. Very few people in the western world would want to experience the life of those lepers, but they would yearn for the spiritual peace and contentment those lepers enjoy.

So how do the guys in Third Day aim to make a difference?

Let me take you back a few years. It's a hot Saturday on the spring leg of the *Come Together* tour. The concert will not start until eight o'clock in the evening, and we have the whole day to do what we want. We're all jammed into the back of a minivan—our destination isn't a ball game, a shopping mall, or a movie theater, or even a bookstore signing session. Instead, we are on the way to a Habitat for Humanity housing project to put in some "sweat equity" and help a family build its new home. A short while later I find myself hammering nails into a piece of wood and then cutting and fitting the wood on the roof of a nearly completed house. We are helping a single-parent mom put the finishing touches on her first-ever home. She'd been working on it herself in her spare time for weeks. David Carr is very good at DIY (Do It Yourself), so he knew exactly how to get started. Most of the others guys were enthusiastic helpers, and Tai roamed around in an advisory capacity, taking lots of pictures.

Later that day when I called home, my wife was amazed that I'd actually done something as practical as helping build a house, because my lack of skill with a hammer, screwdriver, and paintbrush is legendary in our family.

The scene at the Habitat for Humanity house was to be regularly repeated at various locations during the *Come Together* tour and the *Come Together and Worship* tour. The band didn't make a big deal of it. Sometimes the press showed up, and sometimes they didn't. Habitat for Humanity had a booth at every concert, and often we'd see the family we'd been helping that day in the audience of the show. I didn't really need reminding, but the way the guys willingly helped build these houses told me and others that they didn't just talk a good game about using their privileged position to help others, but they actually got up and did it.

We have had the honor of being able to partner with World Vision for almost ten years now. Until just a couple of years ago, none of us in the band had been on a trip to see World Vision in action. Recently, Tai, Mark, and I made our way to a very small country in southern Africa called Lesotho. Since I had never been anywhere in Africa, I had no idea what to expect. I had always pictured myself on just such a trip. For some reason

I imagined that each sponsored child was living in some sort of utopian environment where all of his or her wants and needs were being met. I also assumed that children who had yet to be sponsored were outsiders looking in, just waiting and hoping for their opportunity. How tremendously life altering to be the child living in that rescued oasis. Conversely, how dreadful to be outside the gates with only a hope that someday it could all change. Obviously, my assumptions were wrong. I never really understood the process until I saw it firsthand.

We turned off the highway onto a gravel road that would lead us to a very small village school, visible about a half mile away. Immediately we saw throngs of children pouring out of the school. They recognized the white and orange World Vision pickup trucks and SUVs. As we continued toward the village, the children were running, dancing, singing, shouting, and waving to us. The smiles on their faces and the joy in their eyes are images that will never be forgotten. We stuck our arms out the windows, and they grabbed onto us and wouldn't let go, walking and running beside our vehicles, holding on to our hands and arms and singing joyous welcome songs. I wondered if heaven could have more joy. We spent the next couple of hours with the kids. The children danced and sang songs as we visited their school and the rest of their surroundings and ate a local traditional meal. I was excited to see what World Vision was doing there and in other local villages. Still, I wasn't sure how the process worked.

I started asking questions about benefits of being a sponsored child in comparison to one not yet sponsored. I found out that when World Vision assimilates into a village, the entire community benefits from its efforts. A clean water source is provided for drinking and cooking. The children get to go to school each day and receive a solid meal. Medical services are available. Town meetings are facilitated to open communication and educate adults on farming techniques, social issues, and disease prevention. Ultimately, World Vision acts as the hands and feet of Christ. They meet people and their needs right where they are and exemplify the love of God through service and sacrifice. It is an incredible work that helps meet incredible needs. The more children sponsored in a community, the more resources World Vision has to make a tremendous impact there. We count it an honor to be a part of such an important work being done around the globe, and we continue to challenge our audiences to come alongside this effort to impact the world with the love of Jesus Christ.

Brad Avery, October 2006

One of my earliest memories of Third Day, even before I was actually touring with them, came in Denver on the Newsboys' *Step Up to the Microphone* tour. Arriving in Denver on the Newsboys' bus, I spotted John Poitevent, who was then Third Day's traveling pastor. I asked him where the guys were. He was really pumped up and explained that David, Mac, Tai, Brad, and Mark had decided to take every piece of food on their tour bus—bread, chips, snacks, cookies, cold meats, cheeses, and bottles of water—down to a local park to distribute it to the homeless people in the park. The guys weren't doing this as a publicity stunt, or to appease an organization or ministry, but simply because they had seen a crowd of homeless people and had seen them through the eyes of Jesus. I stored that little incident in my memory banks and often referred to it later when we were discussing living out our faith. During one tour we studied the Book of James together, and here is what the Lord taught us:

A LESSON FROM THE ROAD

FAITH IN ACTION

The book of James helps us discover just how practical our faith is supposed to be. Although there are four men called James in the New Testament, the most likely author of this book is James, the brother of Jesus and leader of the Jerusalem Council. Originally James didn't understand the mission of Jesus and even publicly disagreed with Him, but by the time he writes this book, he has a strong grasp on the idea that faith is as good as dead if it isn't accompanied by action:

> Dear brothers and sisters, what's the use of saying you have faith if you don't prove it by your actions? That kind of faith can't save anyone. Suppose you see a brother or sister who needs food or clothing, and you say, "Well, good-bye and God bless you; stay warm and eat well,"—but then you don't give that person any food or clothing. What good does that do?
>
> So you see, it isn't enough just to have faith. Faith that doesn't show itself by good deeds is no faith at all—it is dead and useless.

Now someone may argue, "Some people have faith; others have good deeds." I say, "I can't see your faith if you don't have good deeds, but I will show you my faith through my good deeds."

Do you still think it's enough just to believe that there is one God? Well, even the demons believe this, and they tremble in terror! Fool! When will you ever learn that faith that does not result in good deeds is useless?—James 2:14–20 NLT

At first glance this passage might appear to be going against the biblical truth that we are saved by faith and not by works, but James doesn't intend to contradict this at all. He is simply saying that acting righteously toward the poor and disadvantaged is the genuine evidence of a saving faith. He exposes the lie that there can be some believers who are just "faith" people and others who are purely "deeds" people.

James challenges us that head knowledge isn't the be-all and end-all. We can be theologically correct and know all the right doctrine, but how consistent are we about transforming theory into practice?

In the times when our faith is challenged and when we see others suffering and in deep need, can we be people who demonstrate faith and love in deeds as well as words?

- Real faith and real love don't display prejudice, selfishness, or favoritism.
- Real faith and real love don't show halfheartedness, apathy, or indifference.
- Real faith and real love take us away from ourselves, our comfortable worlds, and our preoccupations into the suffering and broken world of those around us.
- Real faith and real love are most perfectly demonstrated in the life of Jesus.

James gives us two examples from the Old Testament of people who put their faith into practice. First, he reminds us that Abraham was called a "friend of God" and that the Lord declared Abraham to be righteous. Abraham demonstrated that he was indeed a righteous friend of God when he was willing to sacrifice his son Isaac, proving that his faith and his love for the Lord were real.

The second example James draws to our attention is a surprising one, the prostitute Rahab. James wasn't trying to justify her job, but he tells us that she too was seen as righteous in the eyes of the Lord because of her actions in protecting a bunch of Israelite spies.

The lesson to learn from the writings of James is that our faith must be alive and practical and not just confined to a set of beliefs.

In 2005, Third Day, like all Americans and most people all over the world, was shocked to see the terrible effects of Hurricane Katrina. Almost immediately they knew they should do something to help. Mark Lee takes up the story:

After the tragic events in the Gulf region, we tried to find ways we as a band could get involved. So when KSBJ, a radio station in Houston, contacted us about taking part in its benefit concert for evacuees in that area, we knew this was something we wanted to be a part of. A large number of people have migrated to that area in the wake of Hurricane Katrina, and people in Houston have been responding in a big way. Literally hours after the first evacuees arrived in Houston, KSBJ started a campaign called Cards for Katrina where people could donate gift cards to help out those in need. The goal of Concert for Katrina, which also featured TobyMac, the Crabb Family, and Natalie Grant, was to raise gift cards for this project.

We arrived in Houston early in the afternoon and immediately traveled to the Reliant Center where most of the remaining evacuees were staying. We had the opportunity to help serve lunch at the shelter and then took a brief tour. We got the chance to talk with several people who had been staying there since the hurricane. It is overwhelming to go into situations like this—you don't really know what to say to somebody who's lost so much. All you can do is try to love people and help them think about something else for a while. We all were deeply impacted by this experience.

The concert itself was amazing. Other than Toby, we hadn't seen any of the other artists play live before, so it was fun to watch Natalie Grant's and the Crabb Family's performances. And Toby, as always, totally blew the roof off. Those were some hard acts to follow. Our performance was one we won't soon forget. The crowd was amazing, and we brought out TobyMac and Diverse City and the Crabb Family onstage with us for the encore.

Even better than the concert was the generosity of the fans—3,460 gift cards were collected! Oh, and one last thing. Right before we went onstage, we were presented with a plaque for our humanitarian efforts and were informed that September 19, 2005, was "Third Day Day" in Houston. Now it all made sense. I had noticed that the birds were singing a little louder, the sun was shining a little brighter, and the food even tasted a little bit better. But I couldn't quite put my finger on it. Now I knew why—it was Third Day Day! (I hope you're picking up on the sarcasm here.) Seriously, what an honor that was. And we took it as more of a sign of the generosity of our fans than anything we had done. So thanks again to you, Houston Gomers, for your support and your generosity in making this night a success, and also for your amazing response to the needs brought on by the hurricane.

Mark Lee, Aid Relief Concert, Houston, Texas, September 19, 2005

My personal memory of Houston comes from the fall leg of the *Wherever You Are* tour when on a hot and humid Saturday afternoon I went along with the guys in the band to take part in the Gulu Walk. On Saturday, October 21, 2006, Gulu-Walk Day, we joined over thirty thousand people in eighty-two cities and fifteen different countries as we took to the streets to urge communities to support peace in northern Uganda. The event also raised over fifty thousand dollars for programs that support youth education, training, and child-soldier rehabilitation. The band has been involved with ministry in Uganda for a while, and Tai was able to kick off the walk with a short message of encouragement to the assembled walkers, who included many Gomers. Our leisurely stroll through a downtown Houston park was quite demanding, given the heat and the humidity. It was a stark reminder that thousands of young people walk longer distances every night in northern Uganda simply to find a safe place to sleep. So much of the *Wherever You Are* album was written from a perspective of giving hope to the hopeless, and here Mac explains the album's opening song:

-TUNNEL-

I won't pretend to know what you're thinking
I can't begin to know what you're going through
I won't deny the pain that you're feeling
But I'm gonna try and give a little hope to you

I don't want to sound like a broken record in regard to burdens and hardships, but we play to a lot of people and talk with them afterward, and we realize that everyone carries burdens. None of us have all the answers, but we want to bring a message of hope. It seems that we have trials for one of three reasons:

- We bring them on ourselves because of what we have done or decisions we have made.

- Someone else is bringing them on us.

- They are what God allows us to walk through to draw us closer to Him and make us stronger.

Though we don't have all of the answers, we know who does. So, as we are going though a trial, we have to ask ourselves: Why is it happening? How is it happening? And why is God allowing us to walk through it? And ultimately, how can we grow from it? We know that we don't have all the answers, but we do want to be real. One of the verses says, "I won't pretend to know what you're thinking / I can't begin to know what you're going through." We cannot know what you are going through, but we can bring the hopeful message that there is a light at the end of the tunnel.

Mac Powell

FEELS LIKE I'M
A MILLION MILES AWAY

—SAN ANGELO—

What do you know
And tell me do you have something to say
Don't get me wrong
But I miss my home
And it feels like I'm a million
miles away

I'm starting this chapter sitting in David Carr's fantastic new home in Roswell, Georgia. David is a touch disappointed because he's just found out that the picturesque woodlands surrounding the property will make it impossible for satellite reception, so his TV plans have been thrown into confusion. Before we head off to catch the tour bus tonight for an overnight trip to a summer festival, we both are taking the opportunity to catch up on some work. David's wife has taken their eldest son to the dentist, and their younger son is taking a nap.

One of the great privileges of touring with Third Day is seeing how committed each member is to being a husband and a father. Oftentimes this can be tough with a busy touring schedule. It's a great life being on the road, but it's no fun having a day off in Boise, Idaho, when your family is hundreds of miles away. Nothing personal about Boise, Idaho—it's a good place, but when I've been on the road for two or three weeks, I'd rather be with my wife and family than in a hotel room thousands of miles across the Atlantic!

Anyone who has ever experienced the touring life will tell you that problems with the plumbing, car breakdowns, or family illness always happen when you are away from home—not on your days off! That can be very hard, both for the people on the road and for the people left at home to cope with the situation. I can remember a phone conversation with my daughter, who was in the UK, while I was on a golf course with Brad. She was walking along a street near our house and talking to me over the phone when I heard a loud scream and then a shout of "Watch out!" and then the line went dead. You can appreciate that I was imagining all types of ghastly scenarios made worse by the fact that I couldn't get hold of her on her cell phone for about ten minutes. When I eventually did, she was fine; she had been shouting to a friend to be careful when crossing the road. It has not been easy for the guys to hear that a child is ill or that one of the wives has had a car accident or that there has been a problem with the house while they have had to remain on the road to fulfill another handful of concerts before being able to return home.

It's strange, but I would say that some of the loneliest times of my life have been when I'm traveling from home to meet up with the guys in Third Day. The car trip to the airport and the outgoing flight to the US are the instances when homesickness kicks in, and I have an irrational fear come over me. I know that the Lord will protect my family; I know I will travel safely; I know that the guys in the band will give me a great welcome; but still that fear rises.

I've learned to hand it over to the Lord and not become dominated by it. As soon as I meet up with the band, all is well, and a reassuring call home always helps. It was even more difficult traveling with Newsboys years ago. I didn't have e-mail or a cell phone that worked in the USA, which meant attempting to find a pay phone every other day to stay in touch with my wife.

I often say to folks that the greatest ministry challenge God has given me is to be a good husband and a good father. Knowing all the guys as I do, these roles are at the top of their priority lists, too. As Christian communicators, it's sometimes difficult to live up to the standards we project from the stage; people assume that because we have a public ministry and draw audiences of thousands a night we must be a cross between Billy Graham and the apostle Paul. I've seen enough of Mac, Mark, Tai, Brad, and David in their family settings to tell you two things. First, they aren't perfect! Second, they are men of God genuinely honoring Him in their marriages and in their family life.

Here are some reflections from David:

It's a fairly constant prayer of ours that God would knit us together and bring increasing unity and purpose to our being together. We have heard so often from fans that there is an anointing on Third Day. If that is true, it means that God has put this thing together and that He is the one who sustains it.

It's not always easy to work together, running a ministry and a business, especially one as complex as Third Day. We say all the time that we have the best jobs in the world because we get to make a good living doing what we love to do and also affect the hearts and minds of many people in vast ways.

One interesting observation about Third Day is that if it weren't for the musical common ground and the spiritual calling and direction on the five of us, some of us probably wouldn't have become friends by default. It's not that we don't like each other or appreciate one another's personality or anything like that, but let's face it: we tend to hang out with people of like mind or similar interests more than we do with those who are opposite us. Thankfully, there are the music and our calling to guide us on the same path, because they have taught us, and continue to teach each of us, the importance of majoring on the major things and not on the negative. The positives far outweigh any negatives anyhow. Our wives have a different situation to deal with by default. While they don't dislike each other, there is not as much to bring them together as there is for us in the band. Number one, geographical proximity is a challenge as some of us live an hour, realistically, from one another thanks to the snail-pace crawl of Atlanta traffic. Also, when we get off the road or out of the studio, we all need a break from each other, so the families don't get together very often. I think that is unfortunate, but it's just a reality. It's hard enough to carve out time to hang out with our neighbors sometimes, and they are within walking distance! But our wives all have different personalities, not to mention the fact that they are incredibly tied up with the collective fourteen kids in the Third-Day camp. Again, it's not a matter of dislike or jealousy, but without the umbrella of Third Day, most of our wives would not find themselves hanging out in the same circles of friends.

To be honest, I work harder at home than I do when I'm on the road! I guess that's one of the dangers of touring life: it can become an escape from the reality of everyday life. I want to enjoy life on the road but never forget that I have a family that needs me and that I want to be with.

David Carr, November 2006

In the fall of 2005, we embarked upon a low-key promotional tour for the release of the *Wherever You Are* album, and on our days off I stayed with Mac and his family. This gave me the chance to see how he handled family life. It was so cool to join hands with Mac, his wife, and their children around the dinner table to give thanks for the food, to watch some newly created family movies, and also to see that just occasionally Mac gets a little stressed when driving his family around town! Mac has a great philosophy about watching movies when we are on the road. However much he wants to watch a new release, if it's one his wife would like to see too, he will wait until he's home and take her to see it. During the time I was staying with them, they headed off to see the film about Johnny Cash, *Walk the Line.*

All of the guys much prefer to catch a red-eye flight home to see wives and family on off days on the road rather than have the luxury of a late rise in a hotel room somewhere. When Mark lived in Nashville and I was in town, he and his wife would often welcome me on a family trip out to eat. Their young daughter would always steal the show. It was on one of these occasions that we discovered that we shared the same name for our cats!

Brad and I do a lot of talking on the golf course, and family life is most often the topic. Looking fifteen years or so down the road, Brad sees himself as a professional golfer on a golf course in Florida with his wife in her dream job working at Disney! I'm going to keep in contact with that family—free tickets to Florida golf and to a theme park are too good to miss!

Obviously, God has granted us extreme blessings in our careers to be able to make beautiful music that we enjoy, provide for our families, point others to Him, and ultimately bring honor and glory to His name. However, success is a double-edged sword. On one hand, it affords us the opportunity to enjoy touring on a level that many artists never get to enjoy. On the other hand, it demands more of our time.

On our very first official tour ten years ago, most of us were newlyweds. We had no idea how to manage and protect our time, let alone our barely born marriages. That year we were gone over 250 days from home. We had to learn the lesson the hard way. We formed an accountability board of pastors who could help us maneuver through tough decisions and scheduling demands. We committed to God and our families never to be gone for more than two weeks at a time. It has served us well to put them first—our premier calling. Now ten years later, we get home a couple of days a week during the heavy touring seasons. It may not be the most profitable business model, but it is the plan God has given us to be the best husbands, fathers, friends, and Third Day we can ultimately be.

Brad Avery, October 2006

Most of my touring experiences with Third Day have been very pleasant. I started traveling with the band long after their early days of driving their own trucks and personally loading their own merchandise. My travels have always been on tour buses or planes. Now and then, however, I have begun to think that I'm getting too old for sleeping in a bunk on a bus, even if that bunk does have air conditioning and a DVD player. I can vividly remember driving aimlessly around the city of Belfast in the early hours of the morning in a sleeper bus with our hired driver attempting to find the hotel we were to stay in. The three-hour journey from Dublin became closer to five hours. To make matters worse, we had managed to rent the worst sleeper bus in the UK, one with diesel fumes constantly seeping into the sleeping area and an unusable toilet. At one stage it became so desperate that we considered paying a taxi to drive to the hotel just so the bus driver could follow the cab!

Even more frustrating can be those incidents that happen back at home when we are on the road. It's actually quite easy to slip into a negative mindset when traveling. The big secret to so much of road life, like the Christian journey in general, is all about maintaining a positive attitude and not allowing oneself to become cynical or morose.

Mark Lee is the man who updates Third Day's weblog from the road, so some of his observations and reflections will help give you a sense of the band's perspective about touring life as it really is. Mark wrote regularly on the fall leg of the *Wherever You Are* tour. In the following excerpts you'll see his honesty come through.

First of all, if you ask what we did today, the answer would be basically "nothing." Yup, it's getting to be toward the middle of the tour when you're just trying to grind it out and get through it. When I say that, it has nothing to do with the actual shows. Those have been going quite well. It's just that sort of funk that can set in when you've been away from home a lot over a short period of time. I'm sure it was during one of these times when Mac wrote "San Angelo" with the classic line "though you're surrounded you still feel so alone" (or something like that).

Okay, having said we did nothing, a good deal of things happened, albeit of the somewhat mundane sort. Tai and David got out and enjoyed a nearby greenway trail that featured a visit to Johnny Apple-seed's grave. And we hung out on the bus quite a bit watching college football (Mac's team won, so he was in pretty good spirits) and a new British series Nigel brought out. Speaking of Nigel, he has a lot of ties with Fort Wayne. He's got some friends in the area, and he often speaks at local churches and colleges. One of his good friends, Andy, was here today, so it was cool to hang out with him. Also, our good friend David Mullins and his family were at the show. Nigel led us in another study tonight based on Philippians 1, and we had a great time of prayer before the show.

Mark Lee, October 2006, Fort Wayne, Indiana

Fort Wayne was a significant concert for me because I had so many friends in town, but for the guys in the band it was just another show in the middle of the tour to "grind through."

That's not being disrespectful to Fort Wayne or to the guys in the band, but it's the reality—touring life can sometimes be long and arduous. I'm always amazed that the same show can be fantastic from a guitarist's point of view but be a disaster from the keyboard player's perspective; or it can be a triumph for the vocalist but really difficult for the drummer.

It can be disappointing coming off stage having played to a few thousand people knowing that you've had technical problems or that you simply weren't in the zone. Mark explains much better than I'm able to:

Before I get to the heart of this post, let it be known that we love playing in South Carolina. It was the first place we ever played outside our home state of Georgia, and they've always been very good to us. So if any of the following comments seem negative, it has nothing to do with the fans or the crowd, or even the show as a whole. I just thought you guys might like to hear our side of the picture. Sometimes you leave the stage going, "Wow! That was an amazing show." Sometimes it's more like, "That was a terrible show." Tonight was neither. I think we all left the stage, scratched our heads, and wondered what in the world just happened. There were some excellent moments. Maybe because it's almost the end of the show and we were letting our proverbial hair down, but the acoustic set was expanded to feature our second-ever performance of "Born in Bethlehem." But we didn't stop there. We took requests and found ourselves playing "Give," "Never Bow Down," and even "Rockstar." That would have been awesome. We tried to keep it going and did "Take My Life" instead of "Love Song." Somebody in the crowd tried to start a clap in the middle of the song, and I don't think the song ever found a tempo. And there was some kind of vortex happening on my side

MARK

of the stage. There's an audio term called "out of phase," which means two microphones or sound sources are set up in a fashion where they cancel out each other. I think I was "out of phase" for the better part of the evening. If I zigged, everyone else zagged. It all seemed to start with the first song when my mandolin wasn't working. And it was a downward spiral from there. Sometimes you're the windshield; sometimes you're the bug. Overall, I think it was a fun show, and I think anyone who attended probably had a great time. But in the interest of total access and honesty here, I thought I'd share how it felt from my perspective.

Mark Lee, November 2006, Columbia, South Carolina

In my role as pastor, one of the things I try to do as soon as a concert has ended is to find out from the guys how they think it went and what the general feeling about the show is. Oftentimes what I think has been a great show will only be a good show from the band's perspective (perhaps I'm easily pleased!) Sometimes because I've been in conversation with people backstage on and off during the concert, I'll have totally missed out on the fact that the guys are having a fantastic night! Many of the devotions we share on the road focus on challenging us to rise above the circumstances, whatever they may be, and to seek the Lord's strength to persevere. The real pleasure comes from seeing this happen. Here's Mark again, talking about a concert:

Great show tonight. The day started, like all first shows of a run on this tour, with us flying in from Atlanta. Pretty uneventful flight (good thing), although the weather in both Atlanta and Cincinnati was pretty nasty today. Then it hit us hard before the show that, with all the travel and everything built up over the last few weeks, we were pretty tired. Don't get me wrong—the shows have been awesome. It's everything else that makes it tough. But shows like tonight make me want to keep this tour going indefinitely. The audience was amazing: loud, fun, and, I'll be honest, a little crazy. We stuck to our guns on the set list and played the rocking set we've been doing the last couple of weeks. The thing I'll take away from tonight is the dancing that went on in the first couple of rows and a lot of air guitar too—quite interesting—and the people taking pictures. Someone would run up to the front of the stage, and a couple of us would jump in to pose for pictures with them. It was pretty hilarious.

Mark Lee, November 2006, Cincinnati, Ohio

Touring life can be a strange mix of highs and lows, pleasures and hardships, fun and frustration. In a way it's a microcosm of life itself and especially the Christian journey.

—MOUNTAIN OF GOD—

After all that I've been through
Now I realize the truth
That I must go through the valley
To stand upon the mountain of God

We've all had those mountaintop experiences. You feel so close to God. You can see for miles. Visions galore. Then life happens, the valley, the struggles. We often think that the valley is a consequence for the sin of our life. But maybe it's just our life. We're all promised struggle. We all experience suffering. The hope we have is wonderfully expressed in a line from this song: "You were there with me." We don't have to go through the inevitable trials of life on our own.

Tai Anderson on the song "Mountain of God"

Here's a devotion we shared together on the *Wherever You Are* tour, when we all felt we were running on empty and needed some energy, enthusiasm, and a fresh perspective to help us finish well.

A LESSON FROM THE ROAD

AS THE SPIRIT ENABLED THEM

If I were choosing my team to conquer the world, I'd be looking for intelligent, affluent people with good looks, organizational ability, great communication skills; and I'd be looking for a blend of youth and experience, an ethnic and gender mix; and I'd probably want to throw in musical aptitude and a capacity to connect with a younger generation. When I begin to think like this, two points strike home to me. First, I wouldn't pass my own selection process! Second, I don't think I'd have ever selected the team Jesus did!

I'm always amazed by the way Jesus managed to find a bunch of misfits like the disciples to change the world. He got Matthew, a tax collector for the Romans, to work alongside Simon the Zealot, who wanted nothing more than to do damage to anything Roman! He transformed a bunch of fishermen into fishers of men. He used the hotheaded Peter and the equally thunderous James and John to bring peace into people's lives.

One small, seemingly insignificant phrase helps us understand how the disciples changed from fear to faith, from confusion to courage, from misunderstanding to ministry. In Acts 2 we read the familiar passage about the Holy Spirit coming down from heaven on the day of Pentecost:

> When the day of Pentecost came, they were all together in one place. Suddenly a sound like the blowing of a violent wind came from heaven and filled the whole house where they were sitting. They saw what seemed to be tongues of fire that separated and came to rest on each of them. All of them were filled with the Holy Spirit and began to speak in other tongues as the Spirit enabled them.—Acts 2:1–4 NIV

Without getting drawn into too much theology, I want to focus on the simple words "as the Spirit enabled them." It's these words that help us understand how the disciples were transformed into world changers. God's presence was upon them, and He gave them the power and the ability to carry out the Great Commission.

Andrew preached in what we now call Bulgaria and Georgia and died on a cross in a Greek colony. James the brother of John preached in Judea and was beheaded, while John himself was exiled to the island of Patmos and wrote his gospel. Tradition has it that Thaddeus preached to all of Mesopotamia and was killed by arrows, and after writing his gospel, Matthew was crucified in Alexandria, and Simon the Zealot became the second bishop of Jerusalem. The first bishop was James the brother of Jesus, who was thrown from the temple roof and beaten to death. Nathanael preached in India; Philip preached in Turkey, while both Peter and Thomas ended up preaching to about five significant people groups each, before being killed for their faith.

Now the endings of all those disciples may be quite frightening, but the point is this: God never calls you to a task or a mission without equipping you to carry it out. The Holy Spirit will enable you.

Just as the good news of Jesus didn't end with Jesus, it also didn't end with the disciples. It carries on with us today—we are no less charged with the Great Commission than were those first followers of Jesus. They weren't simply spectators, and neither are we. We are called to serve and to share and to bring light into a dark world. At times we may feel daunted and ill equipped; often we will be tired and discouraged; occasionally we may believe we have little to offer or have been disqualified from the task; but because the Holy Spirit enables us, we can rely on the power of God and not on our own feelings or abilities.

But when the Holy Spirit has come upon you, you will receive power and will tell people about me everywhere—in Jerusalem, throughout Judea, in Samaria, and to the ends of the earth.—Acts 1:8 NLT

On one particular tour we were playing just outside Washington, DC, and the band had an opportunity to go on a guided tour of the White House. Unfortunately, because I was not a US citizen and my details hadn't been submitted well in advance, I wasn't able to enter the White House. The actual wording of the explanation was that I was "an alien," a foreigner in a strange land, which immediately made me think of Third Day's song "Alien," but also reminded me of the fact that I was indeed many, many miles from my home. Sitting in a coffee shop just around the corner from arguably the most famous home in the world (after Buckingham Palace), I reflected on the incredible privileges and opportunities that come with being a touring Christian rock band and also on the sacrifices and challenges that come with this, especially for those of us who are married.

If I felt alien in Washington, DC, that day, the times when I most need to call on the Holy Spirit's power and presence are on my journeys home to the UK. The twenty-four hours before I am due to leave the band and head home are inevitably chaotic with last-chance conversations, decisions, future planning, and a quick dash to a hotel room or an airport. It's often in this process, when I'm physically and spiritually drained, that God offers me divine opportunities to share with people about Jesus. On an overnight flight back from Washington to London, I had been upgraded to business class (a perk of frequent flying) and was sitting next to an American lawyer who was flying on to Iraq to help with the rebuilding of the Iraqi constitution. Bill was a loud, larger-than-life, opinionated, heavy-drinking character who, once he'd heard that I was a Christian, automatically assumed we were direct opposites and had nothing in common. Eight hours later he had changed his opinion. Despite desperately needing some sleep and feeling like I had nothing much left to give after being on the road for five of the previous seven weeks, I conversed with Bill for almost the whole flight; and at one stage we were getting so excited and animated that the passenger in the seat in front had to tell us to keep quiet. A shared love of rock music, Bill's time at an English university as a student, his fondness of many things British, and his strong humanitarian conviction actually gave us many points of reference; and I was able to be an effective spokesman both for the good news of Jesus and for evangelical Christians. Bill was both amused and amazed about the concept of Christian rock music, so I made sure to send a copy of the *Wherever You Are* CD to his office as soon as I was able.

On another occasion I was traveling home from Nashville.

I'd shared a room with David Carr for a night, and we'd talked long into the early hours. Then there came tornado warnings, and being in a room on the tenth floor of a hotel didn't seem like a great idea. When I eventually arrived at the airport on the following day, almost inevitably my flight to Washington Dulles was delayed. Tired, aching, and desperate to go home, I opted for a back and shoulder massage while waiting for the delayed flight when I spotted someone I knew in the massage chair next to me. I had no energy or inclination to even lean over and say hello. Besides, he looked like he was blissfully enjoying his massage, and I didn't want to disturb his enjoyment. Wandering down to the departure gate, I got myself into an antisocial mode in readiness for the journey ahead, only to be asked by a woman carrying about five bags if she'd missed the Washington flight. When I told her it was delayed, she rushed off to the smoking lounge.

Boarding the plane a couple of hours later, I was relieved to see that it looked as though I had an empty seat next to me—just what I needed to stretch out and snooze. The flight attendant told us that they were waiting for one passenger and then we'd be good to go. Now some of you may be ahead of me in this story already. . . yes, you've guessed it; the passenger we were waiting for was the woman who had gone off to the smoking lounge. As she struggled down the aisle with the two large bags she'd managed to bring on, I just knew where she'd be heading—to the empty seat next to me, which I graciously helped her into after stowing her bags in the overhead bins. Now I had a choice ahead of me. Actually, I had a few options: I could ignore her and get some sleep, I could engage in some lighthearted chat as she was actually quite an attractive

125

person, or I could trust God and open up a more meaningful dialogue. Fortunately, the Holy Spirit prompted me to do the latter, and after exchanging some small talk and finding out why we both had been in Nashville and where we were traveling to, the conversation took on a spiritual dimension.

The woman named Irene was half Norwegian and half Greek and had parents who were involved with a Christian relief agency working in the Middle East and Africa. Before too long she confided in me that she didn't believe she was good enough to serve God in the way that her parents and I did, and that in many ways she felt she was lost and without purpose in life. In fact, if I were searching for someone to ask the optimum questions to begin talking about the good news of Jesus, Irene was that person! I began to encourage her that God loves lost people and told her the stories of the lost son and the lost sheep. I explained that although she thought smoking, drinking, and other lifestyle issues meant she wasn't good enough for God, actually none of us were good enough for God and that He judges us by the state of our heart, not just our outward actions. I was able to describe to her how the death, resurrection, and new life of Jesus had changed my own life and given me forgiveness, faith, power, and purpose. Irene listened intently and readily accepted my suggestion that I send her a book to read. I'd thought that *Purpose Driven Life* by Rick Warren would be a great help to her and promised to send it to her if she e-mailed me her address.

As we prepared to depart from the plane at Washington Dulles, two surprising things happened. First, the young guy in the seat ahead of us waited to speak to me as we walked off. He'd heard every word of our conversation and wanted to thank me for being so inspirational. He was a youth pastor returning from the very conference in Nashville where Third Day had been performing and had never had the courage to witness to someone on a plane. I was very humbled and imagined what he would have been thinking if I'd just engaged Irene in small talk for the whole flight or worse still had tried to mildly flirt with her. Second, I realized that *Purpose Driven Life* was very likely to be available in an airport bookshop, so I rushed off to find a shop and the book. Thirty minutes later I was making my way to the departure gate for the Munich flight because Irene was flying there on her way to Athens. I'd arrived at the gate before she did (remember she was carrying a load of bags), and as she approached the gate, I was standing there nervously clutching *Purpose Driven Life* in a brown paper bag. I explained to her about buying the book, handed it over to her for some reading on the flight to Munich, and asked her to e-mail me with her observations about the book once she had read a few chapters. Irene was overcome by the moment, amazed that a complete stranger would buy her a book and search her out at the airport in order to give it to her. With a tear in her eye she hugged me, and we went our separate ways. A week or so later I got an e-mail from Irene. In it she said this:

> *I wish to thank you for the book and the effort you made to give it to me! To me an experience like that proves that there is a God! I guess God does these actions to remind us that he is around! I have read four chapters and I find it very peaceful and soothing for my precious little soul!*

It's likely Irene and my paths may never cross again, but I

firmly believe that on April 3, 2006, God brought us together on that flight so that He could use me to share something of the love and hope of Jesus with her. I'm so glad I rose above tiredness and my self-centeredness and managed to be obedient to the prompting of the Holy Spirit.

Most times a Third Day tour will finish in Atlanta. Sometimes I'm at the Atlanta show, and sometimes I'm not, depending on my schedule and available flights. The Atlanta concert is a homecoming for the guys, with family, friends, and members of their churches packing out the audience. It's always a highlight, but quite draining too—coming at the end of a tour. Here's a reflection from Mark Lee written in Alabama the day before the last show of the *Wherever You Are* tour:

Tai made a great point right after the show tonight that this could have been the best show we've ever had. Think about it. If it was the best show of this tour, and we're all confident that this is the best tour we've ever done, then this was our best show ever. All that is debatable, but let it be known that tonight was one of *those* kinds of shows. Before I get to that, let me fill you in a bit on what we've been up to today.

We had a long haul and didn't get in until about ten this morning. We watched some of the bonus footage from *Slingblade* on the bus. In case you were wondering, that's one of our collective favorite movies. Then we did an extended interview with American Family Radio. The afternoon was spent watching the Iron Bowl. It was cool to be in the state of Alabama to witness (on TV at least) one of the classic rivalries in college football. It didn't go Mac's way, but it was still cool. Then we rehearsed for the upcoming Thanksgiving event we were doing in Atlanta the next week.

That night we featured a slight change right at the beginning. We opened with "'Til the Day I Die." We weren't expecting much of a response—we were just doing it for us. But the crowd was *way* into it. That let us know that this was a great crowd and that it was going to be a special night. That feeling just seemed to grow with every song. By the acoustic set, it was really happening, and by the end of the main set, it was definitely on.

During the encore someone held up a sign for us to play "Rockstar." You know the deal: if you hold up a sign, we might play your request. So we played it. And it was amazing. Thank you, Alabama. I'll be honest—we were more than a little surprised. When we saw this show on the list of cities, we weren't expecting much. But you guys showed up in a major way. I don't know why we expected any less. You guys are amazing. Tomorrow marks the last day of the tour. It's a bittersweet feeling, and it will be fun to finish strong in our home city. But let me tell you, it will be next to impossible to top tonight.

Mark Lee, November 2006, Mobile., Alabama

THIS IS THE BODY

-COMMUNION-

This is the body
This is the blood
Broken and poured out
For all of us

Changi International Airport in Singapore must be the best airport in the world. It has a swimming pool, a golf course, two hotels, a well-equipped gym, and hundreds of shops all just in the transit area. It's an airport most people visit on their way to somewhere else, and here in January 2007 I'm no different. I'm sitting in a departure lounge and waiting for a flight to Melbourne in order to meet Third Day and their crew for a series of concerts in Australia and New Zealand. It's been a mammoth journey for me, commencing by leaving home on Saturday evening and eventually meeting the band on Tuesday morning. We'll be doing four concerts in six days, with travel every day, so we'll be tired but determined to serve the body of believers in Melbourne, Sydney, Brisbane, and at the Parachute Festival in New Zealand. When we toured Australia and New Zealand two years ago, it was a special time with some memorable concerts, especially at Hillsong in Sydney. Now refreshed after a stopover in Singapore, I'm ready for action. Even after years of doing this, I'm still thrilled at the opportunity to minister alongside and to Third Day, to meet Christians from different parts of the world, and to be reminded that the body of Christ here on earth is immense. I take seriously the privilege of my role as road pastor and place a high priority on "body life"—interacting together as followers of Jesus.

In the introduction to this book, I mentioned the two questions everyone asks me when first finding out that I travel with Third Day as their road pastor. The first question is, "How did you get the job?" And the second question is, "Can I come and carry your bags?" If people ask a third question it is most often, "What exactly do you do as a road pastor?" It's a great question and one I'll attempt to answer now.

All of the guys in the band, and their families, are involved in local churches back in the Atlanta area; and all of them have close Christian friends and church leaders they look up to. My role is simply to help the band, and sometimes the crew, have church on the move as we travel from city to city across America.

—KEEP ON SHININ'—

Despite all your tendencies, God sees
it differently
Your struggle's a time to grow
And you, you're a miracle, anything
but typical
It's time for the whole wide world to
know

When we first started touring, it was a rare Sunday that we would be able to attend our home churches. As we've attempted to balance our home and road lives over the last couple of years, we've made it a point not only to attend church whenever we get the chance but also to be actively involved in what's going on. If you've been even remotely paying attention, it's apparent that God has been doing some cool things through the church over the last couple of years. This song is a song of encourage-

MARK

ment to the church, both as a whole and to the average person sitting in the pew on Sunday morning.

The first verse focuses on the church at large. I recently read a book by Hugh Hewitt entitled *The Embarrassed Believer.* In it he points out that there are literally millions of people attending church in a given week and that the culture should be feeling the effects of that. In the years since the book was published, we've seen many brave souls look for new ways to take the gospel beyond church boundaries. This is where the "millions of voices singing new choruses" line comes into play. Yet sometimes it's "easier said than done." Life happens. Things don't work out as we planned. Like John Lennon said, "Life is what happens to you while you're making other plans."

It's easy at times like these to beat ourselves up and throw in the towel. But if we could see ourselves as God sees us, we'd know that we don't give ourselves nearly enough credit. In God's eyes, we're "a miracle, anything but typical." Faith is a response to God's love for us. When you realize that He sees us in that light and loves us unconditionally, it makes you want to "keep on shinin'" wherever you are or whatever you're going through.

Mark Lee

The band prays together every night before a show, and often we'll spend some time in a Bible study or discuss a devotional book we've been reading. Normally these studies are in our dressing room or on the band tour bus, and most times the only people present will be the guys you see on stage in the band and me. Occasionally there might be others present— personal friends, management or record-company people, or other musicians or baseball players from that locality. On one memorable instance in Chicago on the *LiveWire* tour we welcomed seven of the Atlanta Braves onto the bus for our Bible study and prayer time together.

Often I will spend informal time with one or more of the guys—in a mall or a coffee shop with Tai and David, at a ball game with Mac and Mark, or on the golf course with Brad. I can imagine you are already feeling great sympathy for me as you read this! Seriously though, life on the road can be lonely and days can be long, so quality friendship and uplifting conversation can be very important. Here Brad tells us how he maintains his devotional life on the road:

Many of our fans ask how we keep focused on God out on the road. I think there is an assumption that our time is consumed with media, retail, fans, and sound checks. What most people don't know is that our lives on the road are very structured. They have to be. We actually have tremendous amounts of downtime that require activities and hobbies to help us endure. Schedules and consistency are important in all daily routines to help maintain balance and sanity. With this in mind, it is almost easier for us to keep our focus and attention on God on the road than at home. Home life tends to have more distractions and surprises that take away from a consistent routine and time in devotion. With wives, kids, friends, e-mail trails, and "honey-do's," time alone to press in to God can be hard to find.

We know we have a tremendous responsibility to God and His calling in our lives. We also know we are accountable to each other, families, friends, and fans to always pursue a growing and mature relationship with the Creator. "To whom much is given, much is required." We honor that calling and want to continue to hear what God would have for our lives, ministry, and career.

I tend to enjoy spending time alone with God first thing in the morning when I wake up. It seems to be the quietest time on the bus and helps me focus my heart and mind before the day's requirements commence. I usually begin by welcoming God to be a part of my entire day and worshiping Him. Then I spend time reading Scripture and contemplating what I've read. With God's Spirit as my guide, I can work through thoughts, feelings, and emotions. Finally, I spend time in prayer, confessing my sin, giving thanks for God's abundant blessing and answers to prayer, and interceding for family and friends.

I am always blessed to be able to carve out time with God, and I know that He joins me there in those quiet moments.

Brad Avery, October 2006

One of my main priorities on the road is to ensure that, if we have a concert on a Sunday, we find time to have a short church service together. It's rarely possible because of traveling and time constraints that we actually get to a local church on the road, so normally we will share a Communion service for band, crew, management, and local tour personnel sometime on a Sunday afternoon. I have a very special memory of the Communion service at a show on the *Come Together and Worship* tour with Third Day, Michael W. Smith, and Max Lucado. It was memorable for two reasons: first, because Max Lucado was gracious enough to suggest that he and I share the tour devotional responsibilities. The humility of that world-famous author and speaker was amazing. He encouragingly sat in on my devotions a couple of times a week, just as I enthusiastically sat in on the ones he led for band and crew.

The second reason was that when I was leading the Communion service we happened to be at West Point Military Academy. The guys in Third Day gathered, with Michael and his band, Max, and a number of officer cadets who had been assigned to help us during the day. As I prayed over the bread and the Communion wine (actually it was grape juice borrowed from catering!), I noticed two people rise gently from their seats, position themselves on either side of me and get ready to act as my Communion stewards and hand out the bread and the wine. I looked up, and Michael W. Smith was to my right and Max Lucado was to my left. Both quietly took the bread and wine and began to serve assembled members of the tour. Michael and Max are both legendary figures in modern Christianity, but that day at West Point, their humility as members of the body of Christ and their servant-hearted nature as followers of Jesus shone through.

Two of the songs on the *Wherever You Are* CD were inspired by the movie *The Passion of the Christ*: "Communion" and "Carry My Cross." I wanted to have a song that served as a reminder of the sacrifice Jesus had gone through and our need for that sacrifice. That's where "Communion" came from. Musically, we wanted to write this song as a tool for the church to use in worship. It was meant to be a simple song (just one verse) that could be used in churches, Bible studies, or cell groups with just a guitar or a piano and a few chords or notes, so everyone could worship together. The song makes me think of the story in John 17 where Jesus was in the garden before He was crucified. He prayed to the Father to unite His followers together and to Himself, just as He and His Father are united. So, when we participate in Communion, we not only unite with the Father, but also come together with our brothers and sisters in communion.

MAC

Mac Powell

It's good to bring yourself back to the cross and the resurrection of Jesus time and time again. On the early part of the *Wherever You Are* tour we studied what it meant to be people of the cross. I shared a similar devotion at the Gomer Gathering in Nashville in April 2006.

A LESSON FROM THE ROAD

PEOPLE OF THE CROSS

One day when Jesus was alone praying, He called His disciples to Him and asked them who they thought He was. Then He gave them this warning:

"The Son of Man must suffer many things and be rejected by the elders, chief priests and teachers of the law, and he must be killed and on the third day be raised to life."
Then he said to them all: "If anyone would come after me, he must deny himself and take up his cross daily and follow me. For whoever wants to save his life will lose it, but whoever loses his life for me will save it."—Luke 9:22–24 NIV

On a later occasion He said to the gathered crowd:
"And anyone who does not carry his cross and follow me cannot be my disciple."—Luke 14:27 NIV

So if we are going to be people of the cross, what will we be like?

—A PERSON OF DISTINCTIVENESS

It must have been common in Israel to see condemned men carrying their cross beams out of town to be crucified along the roads; Jesus worked in the timber trade, so he must have known all about crosses. The man who carried a cross did so under condemnation. He had already been found guilty; he was an outcast, an outsider. So perhaps Jesus is saying that to follow Him we will have to stick out like sore thumbs, we will have to be different from the crowd. But perhaps we don't want to be different; perhaps we'd rather not carry a cross; perhaps we'd rather blend in than stick out. Yet following Jesus is going to be difficult; we might be ridiculed, made to look stupid carrying our cross.

I sometimes worry about the desire some Christians have to be so culturally relevant that they are afraid to be different and aren't willing to stick out like a sore thumb on occasions. To have an impact on this society we need to be relevant, but most of all we must be different and accept all the hardships that being different might encompass. How far are we prepared to merge with popular culture without beginning to compromise our faith? Remember that Jesus, of course, was constantly being criticized for getting too much into everyday life; however, he was remembered and noted for being unrivaled, unparalleled, unprecedented, and unique.

Jesus talked about narrow gates and broad gates; His way was the narrow one. He talked about camels going through the eye of a needle. Many are called but few are chosen. Following Jesus as our leader is going to be tough.

—A PERSON OF SACRIFICE

The cross was often carried by rebel slaves; so when Jesus tells us to carry our cross, He makes sure we understand the type of people we must identify with: the weak, the poor, the oppressed, those who are fighting for freedom. As Christians we are called to make a difference in this world and make our primary concern be for others and not for ourselves. A Christianity that only talks about what we get out of it ourselves is unbalanced. We must stand up for justice, peace, and love. If we experience those things in our own lives because of the grace of God, our response must be to go out to others who have been forced to carry a cross, whatever it is.

The apostle Paul was prepared to be "the scum of the earth, the refuse of the world" so that the gospel would be preached (1 Corinthians 4:13 NIV). He was so compelled by the love of God that he didn't care if people thought he was mad or sane. If we live a Christian life with the emphasis purely on what others think of us, with endless energy and activity, we miss the point that a personal relationship, not public usefulness to others, is central to the kingdom.

Oswald Chambers, the great Bible teacher, preacher, and writer of the early twentieth century, says this in his book *My Utmost for His Highest*:

> It is one thing to follow God's way of service if you are regarded as a hero, but quite another thing if the road marked out for you by God requires becoming a doormat under other people's feet. . . . Are you ready to be sacrificed like that? Are you ready to be less than a mere drop in the bucket—to be so totally insignificant that no one remembers you even if they think of those you served? Are you willing to give and be poured out until you are used up and exhausted?
>
> By ignoring the invitation of Jesus to take up your cross, you may become more prosperous and successful from the world's perspective, and you'll have more leisure time and will be more in control of your own life. But are you content with that, or are you prepared to take up your cross? If you are ready to be a dis-

ciple and to sacrifice yourself, then you must be ready to accept the consequences as they come, without complaints in spite of what God might send your way. (Dodd, Mead, & Company, 1935)

—A PERSON ON A JOURNEY

It's so important to remember that when we become Christians, it is not the end of our journey of faith but rather just the start. Every day should be an adventure; every day should bring a new challenge. We should be constantly growing as we journey nearer to our eternal destination with the Lord.

Jesus says, "Come, follow me," and that means going against the flow. As the saying goes: Any old dead fish can float downstream, but it needs life and determination to swim against the tide! We'll be able to discover God's presence in the hardest times and in the most difficult places in life. We'll carry our crosses daily as if each day were our last, each day symbolizing death and new life.

So taking up my cross means being exceptional in the ordinary things of life and being holy on the ordinary streets, among ordinary people.

—A PERSON WITH A MESSAGE

I know very well how foolish the message of the cross sounds to those who are on the road to destruction. But we who are being saved recognize this message as the very power of God.
—1 Corinthians 1:18 NLT

The message of Jesus is, above all, good news! Yet so often Christians sound as if we are bad news. We become known for all the things we are against and all the issues we oppose. Instead, we should be messengers of hope, forgiveness, and redemption.

—A PERSON OF VICTORY

The cross of shame and pain is also the cross of resurrection and the cross of victory. The apostle Paul confirms this for us: "How we thank God, who gives us victory over sin and death through Jesus Christ our Lord!"—1 Corinthians 15:57 NLT

And when we have carried our cross here on earth, we have a crown waiting for us in heaven: "God blesses the people who patiently endure testing. Afterward they will receive the crown of life that God has promised to those who love him."—James 1:12 NLT

—CARRY MY CROSS—

So I'll carry my cross
And I'll carry the shame
To the end of the road
Through the struggle and pain
And I'll do it for love
No, it won't be in vain

We all have crosses to carry. Maybe it's the guilt of sin. Maybe it's a loss or temptation. Maybe it's a personal or emotional affliction. The weight of those burdens can keep us paralyzed. Jesus carries them for us. But that's not all. Though we will always have struggles, God gives us not just another burden. God gives us a yoke that is light. We can sign up with His kingdom and be a part of the incredible tale of human history with a unique and meaningful purpose.

Tai Anderson, on the song "Carry My Cross"

On a couple of occasions I've gone to church with Tai and his family. The first time he suggested this was on the Saturday night of the U2 show in Atlanta. Sunday morning my cell phone rang at 8:45 AM, and I was still in bed. Tai informed me I had forty minutes or so to get showered, borrow a car from Mac (I was staying with Mac), get directions to the Anderson house, and head over for church. I managed it in time and went along with Tai to Sunday school and then to the worship service. As we walked along a corridor in the church, we peeked into the children's session to see Tai's wife acting in the drama. Oftentimes Tai and I had engaged in conversations about the local church, and he's been willing to share his thoughts here:

I'm writing a very different story here than I would have a year or two ago. To be honest, I've never been all that involved in my local church. In high school, I attended a youth group that had a significant role in shaping my life. (My youth pastor also had a fundamental role in me being in Third Day.) But as an adult, church has been more of an exercise of obligation rather than an integral part of who I am.

When my wife and I were looking for a place to get married, we stumbled upon the church we now attend. The church has a pitifully unbeautiful sanctuary and would have been a terrible place to have our wedding ceremony, but the secretary was really nice. You see, as we were visiting different sanctuaries one week to find our wedding chapel, we were told all about the different buildings, stained glass, hardwood floors, and flower arrangements. But it was only at my current church that anyone asked us about ourselves. The secretary congratulated us on our engagement and invited us to Sunday services. So, we came back. Then another simple little miracle happened. A couple introduced themselves to us and invited us to a Sunday school class. We had visited other churches where I felt guilty even taking up a parking space, so it was nice to feel welcome. That day we met some of our closest friends with whom we have now spent a good portion of our lives. We began a process that has tied us in communal experiences with a network of other families as we all are doing our best to raise our kids together.

Fast-forward eight years or so, and you won't find me quite so glowing about the whole operation. Though we had a very tight circle in our small communal group, Sunday services were leaving me feeling pretty flat. Like a lot of churches, my church was going through a pastoral change. This would be the second one since we started attending, and it was getting old. During this process, we would hear from any number of speakers on any given Sunday. Now, as a baseline, I travel a lot! So, I probably only make it to church about twenty times a year at most. During those visits, I was beginning to feel as if I never heard from the same pastor twice, and I was finding it hard to connect. But all that was just the surface of a major spiritual issue that was lurking underneath.

I really didn't value the local church. As a member of a successful Christian band, doing the work of ministry myself, I had seen it all. We'd met Billy Graham at a stadium crusade with fifty thousand attendees. I had been "backstage" of almost every denomination in the country, and I'd seen a good bit of the Christian experience in other parts of the world. I felt above it all. I'm being honest here, so let criticism fly as it will. But at the time, no one was being critical. I was in Third Day! We toured with Max Lucado; we had a pastor who traveled with us on the road; we pray before every show; we're always doing some sort of Bible study or reading something together. Furthermore, I had already been to Africa twice and was feeling the beginnings of a big draw toward the church's role as an advocate for social justice. I wasn't hearing that on Sunday morning. My church looked like another rich, white, suburban country club. So, I began to check out. Church was something good for my wife when I was on the road. Church was good for my kids. I paid my tithe with all the enthusiasm I pay local sales tax, but emotionally and spiritually I invested far less than even 10 percent.

In the summer of 2005, a trip to the UK began to change all that. At the end of our run through England, Wales, Ireland, and Northern Ireland, we had a final show in Scotland. There we shared the stage with two bands for which I have enormous respect: Delirious? and Newsboys. At the hotel after the show, I had a rare chance to hang out with some of the guys in Delirious? and specifically Martin Smith. (It was my birthday, and at some point during the night a bagpipe player walked through the lounge we were in and played "Happy Birthday," surely waking up every guest in the hotel, but that's a different story!) As I was getting to know Martin, who is, without a doubt, one of the most brilliant songwriters and leaders of the modern worship movement, all of his conversation and all of his enthusiasm kept coming back to his local church. Here was a guy who had sung in stadiums, and he was most passionate about singing at his church the following weekend. File that away.

Then, on the trip back to the US we were on the same flight as the Newsboys. When we landed in Chicago, Mac and I ate lunch with

Peter Furler. We've known Peter for years because we opened up for the Newsboys on tour to support both of our first two records. I've always had immense respect for Peter as a shaper of our industry with an incredible business mind and passion for music. But as we sat across the table from him at Chili's, all he could talk about was his local church, its emphasis on missions, and his passion for this communal network of believers. During our lunch, he directly and specifically challenged me to get more involved in my local church.

About a week after my return from the UK tour, I was to speak at a men's breakfast at my church. I've gotten a little more accustomed to it over the years, but as a rule, dread speaking at these things. I've heard some great speakers over the years, so I always feel horribly inadequate, and then there's the problem of actually having something to say. Well, the upshot of speaking gigs is that they drive you to your knees. There I was, locked in my study, Bible open, Internet search engine humming, trying to think of something meaningful to say to this group of mostly older men from my church who would come to hear me speak. I had nothing, so I thought I'd give God a chance to pipe in.

Over the course of that week, God slowly but deliberately convicted me of the unbiblical and errant way I was living my life. The breakdown was simple. Like a bad spy movie, I was living a double life that God (and my wife) could see right through. There was "Third Day Tai," and then there was "Home Tai." On the road, I was a Super Christian who was passionate about Africa, committed to supporting youth ministry, and a leader of worship. At home, I slid into the back of the service and headed for the car as soon as I could grab the kids out of Sunday school. I wasn't talking to anyone about my experiences in Africa. I wasn't having any impact on the youth in my own community, and my only addition to morning worship was that of a music critic. Who needs that? In firm rebuke, God was calling me toward adulthood, spiritual maturity, and consistency. It was high time that I started being the same person on the road and at home. It was time to stop criticizing the church and start participating.

My men's breakfast talk ended up being much more of a confession and invitation to the men of my church to hold me accountable as a fellow man, not as some celebrity Christian. Last year, I had a discipleship group of six high school seniors I did my best not to totally screw up right before they headed off to college. I've also found some incredible core relationships, including one with the young adults pastor who has also felt God's calling to and passion for Africa. In addition, I have a direct and meaningful relationship with our new pastor, who is one of the few African American pastors on the north side of Atlanta and is already impacting great change and movement toward better diversity in our congregation.

I'm not at the end of this road. My church isn't perfect, and neither is yours. But I can honestly tell you that my church home is shaping and impacting me more now than I ever imagined possible. I'm excited about a future not only where I receive sound teaching, but also where I hope I am having an impact as part of a body of believers being perfected to our ultimate role and calling as a beautiful bride—but with the callused hands of a carpenter.

Tai Anderson, October 2006

One of the things I've learned about the Christian music industry is that it is very difficult to be a part of it and really flourish without being involved in a local church. You may be able to get away with it for a year or two, an album or two, a tour or two; but, ultimately, being in public ministry will become too demanding, and your spiritual life will diminish, without being plugged into local church. I firmly believe that Third Day would never have lasted as long as they have without a devotional focus on the road and a commitment to local church when they are home. Both of these priorities don't come without some sacrifice and some discipline.

Mac often lets me stay with him and his family on short breaks from touring. On one memorable occasion he invited the pastors of his church to join us for an evening together. The evening demonstrated that Mac values his church and his pastors, and he was thrilled that I was able to meet them. I'll let Mac tell his "church" story:

My family and I have been at our local church for the last seven years, and we love it. If the hardest thing about touring is leaving family behind, then I think the second hardest is being away from our church. That's why we take people such as Nigel on tour with us, so that we can have church on the road.

I love my local church and the people there. In seasons when Third Day is at home or off the road, I really enjoy being part of and contributing to the life of our church. Sometimes it's been a challenge getting a houseful of children ready for church and taking them into Sunday classes, especially if I've only just arrived home early Sunday morning on the tour bus. Whenever we really take the time and spend the energy going, it's always worth it, and we get something out of being there.

Outside of the band, my closest friends are either people I met growing up in church or people who go to the same church as we do now. My wife has five really close female friends; they all grew up together in church and still enjoy that friendship. As a result, I often get together with their husbands, who have become good friends to me.

Mac Powell, November 2006

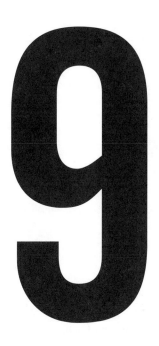

LORD OF ALL CREATION

—GOD OF WONDERS—

Lord of all creation
Of water, earth, and sky
The heavens are Your tabernacle
Glory to the Lord on high

A lot of times we make the album, and then in hindsight we look back and see what the common themes are. But with *Wherever You Are*, things were different. We didn't want to force an overall theme, but without sounding too spiritual about it, I believe that God was at work in the album development. Mark, Brad, and I wrote songs separately; but as we came together and shared the ideas in the studio, we noticed that almost all of the songs had a common theme of hope through adversity. Normally we allow what's in our hearts to come out in the lyrics, so it was obvious that God had been planting the same feelings in us all.

Mac Powell, November 2006

Having listened to Christian music for well over twenty-five years, my observation is that Christian musicians are not always as creative as they could be. There is much pressure to produce the Christian equivalent of what is successful in the charts rather than pursuing originality; and Christian lyrics, in an attempt to communicate the unchanging message of the gospel, can come across as clichéd and jaded. However, I believe that none of these criticisms can be leveled at Third Day. While undoubtedly they have been influenced by others, I have long marveled at the distinctive and original style of both the music and the lyrics the band has come up with over the years. While some Christian artists chose to ride the "worship explosion" with albums packed with covers of recent popular worship songs, the guys of Third Day have chosen to write fresh worship songs or cover existing but little-known songs they felt deserved a wider hearing. This chapter will take us behind the creative process and confirm that we worship a creative God who gives us the talent to create for ourselves and to bring Him glory.

You might think that a drummer would be the least involved in a band's creative processes, but that isn't necessarily true. Here's David Carr's view of how an album comes together:

Working on a new album is like a snowball effect. You start with very little, but you build on it and build on it. Someone brings a rough idea for a song, someone else suggests a chorus, someone else will throw in a guitar riff, and we build a song from there. Fast-forward to a bookstore signing session, and I'm holding a copy of the finished album all packaged up! I think, "How the heck did we get to this?" But we always do. If you think about it, even the greatest albums of all time start with one or two guys having an idea. We start with songwriting sessions when guys bring lyrics to the rest of us, and we work out how we want to develop these as songs and how we will record them. Then we go into the studio, the creative environment, and begin to lay down the songs. Perhaps in the future, we might be bolder and go straight into the studio and create a really tight and strong album but not spend so much time.

When someone brings a song into the band, he always holds it loosely and allows the rest of us to comment and make suggestions. I have never taken a song into that situation, and for a while it bothered me. I thought, "Okay, I'm going to be a songwriter," so I sat in my basement with a guitar and the six chords I know and thought, "Mac can do this with three chords, so I should be able to write a song!" Very soon I realized that my motivation wasn't from wanting to write, but it was coming from pride and from a desire for financial gain. I felt sleazy about trying to write worshipful songs to God when what I was really seeing were dollar signs.

As far as drum parts go, when I hear a song, I'm immediately thinking about that. Usually, I go with my first instincts, my gut reaction to a song, and develop my drum parts from there. Sometimes when we demo a song, it sounds stronger and grittier than the finished product.

David Carr, November 2006

When the finished product is eventually released, it's definitely a crucial time for the band. In many ways, it's like the birth of a new baby, so who better to describe the feelings that surround a new album than Tai Anderson:

Today is the day for which we've been waiting for nine months—it's the launch of our new album *Wherever You Are*. As a father of five, I can certainly relate. A lot of anticipation can grow over nine months. Even though we've been living with this album for a few months now, if our fans don't like it, well???

It gets more difficult with more records. You'd think it would get easier. But it's almost as if the expectations grow for each album. Early this summer, a pastor shared an old quote with us: "Expectations are often premeditated resentments." I'm trying not to look at this record that way. It would be easy for me to assign a number of sales to this record as a signifier of success. However, I'm not going to do it. Instead, I just feel anticipation, because I honestly think the success of this record is going to be wrapped up in the individual lives that are impacted by the message of hope it contains.

Being in Atlanta on the day the album released meant that my day started with me dropping off my son at kindergarten. Then, it was off to meet a friend who had borrowed my Avalanche to pick up some wood from Home Depot. About 9:45, I met my buddy at the only place where people meet anymore: Starbucks. Then I was off to Earthlink Live. I could have gone down earlier and been a part of the CNN interview, but lately I've had a serious case of foot-in-mouth disease. So Mark graciously agreed to cover for me. I got to the venue at 10:15 and began setting up my stuff and checking out our new lighting toys. That kept me busy until noon when Mac and Mark returned from CNN and we started a sound check. This was our first live show with Scotty Wilbanks. He's played on all of our records except our first two, so we know him well. But *live* is always a different animal from in the studio. No pressure though, it's just a packed house! Oh yeah, and two hundred radio stations! Oh yeah, and that pesky Internet!

Well, Scotty was prepared. I know comparisons and contrasts to Geof will be inevitable. But, to me, it was just fresh. There's always a different feeling when you're making music with different people. There's a new sense of excitement and even nervousness that make it new for everyone. We practiced all day! As I write this, my back is actually a bit sore from wearing that heavy bass all day. We got the music to a good place. It will always take us a few weeks to be totally dialed in. After rehearsal, we had only an hour before the show. There were a lot of people to meet: all the folks at Chevy who were making this event happen and all the folks from the record company and management. Don McCollister, who engineered the record, was in a separate studio at Earthlink Live to mix for the broadcast. I was saying "hey" to some old friends, and my wife called to tell me that she was on her way down.

Last time we were at Earthlink Live, we played a sales conference for *Wire*, and afterward, my wife backed up our Tahoe into a pole underneath the building. So today she was forbidden to drive. I'm not sexist, just practical. She came down with some friends. I'm always anxious to make sure my wife and friends make it safely inside. With about twenty minutes to spare, everyone had arrived. I went into the dressing room to get ready, and there was Mac lying down on his back and saying over and over again, "I don't got it." These rehearsal/show days are pretty hard on Mac's voice, and he was starting to feel that dreaded sore throat, sinus, tired feeling. No bird flu though, so the show goes on. We huddled up and prayed for the show. The show was different as the audience became more of a studio audience, and there were a few weird pauses. But I was pretty excited about the music. One song in particular really did it for me, "I Can Feel It." I actually hit a few wrong notes at the end of the song, but I was going for it. The song has a great build and anticipation to it.

After the concert, I kissed my wife goodbye, shook some hands, and signed some autographs. By "some" I mean several hundred people in a long line. I was toast or "cream-crackered," as we like to say. (We learned that one from Nigel.) I had a bad case of the yawns but was trying not to be rude to all the folks who had been waiting in line. After it was over and a couple of wrong turns later, Mac and I crashed in a hotel room. We were doing morning radio, so there was no point in going home just to turn around and come back downtown in the morning. It would have taken thirty minutes to get home at night, but ninety minutes to get back in the morning through Atlanta rush-hour traffic. We got a lot more sleep staying downtown. It was a strange feeling to be in Atlanta and not staying at home. All in all, it was a great day. We pulled off the music. We were "on" for the fans, and our new album was on the streets.

Tai **Anderson**, November 1, 2005, Atlanta, Georgia

You already know that on the road, one of the main gathering points offstage for the band is our devotional time together. However, there is another fairly regular gathering time when we get together to enjoy the creativity of other people. We seldom think of it in those terms, and in reality, it's more about relaxation, but whenever we get the opportunity, most of us will head off to a movie theater. Before going to bed on the bus, we may all watch an episode of the latest TV show or laugh together at a sitcom DVD. We may even tune the satellite to a music channel and watch a documentary or live concert recording of a rock band.

Whatever it is, we have learned to enjoy the creativity of others—certainly not indiscriminately because we can spot a "turkey" quicker than almost anyone! I'm constantly amazed by how much inspiration the guys in the band get from seeing the top-quality work of others. For my part, I'm able to bring some new British comedy DVDs over with me, and I take great pride in introducing them to anyone who cares to watch!

A few years ago a man named Peter Brind joined our Ignite team in Cardiff. Peter had been a biology teacher for many years but was also involved in leading a church in Cardiff. His role with Ignite was to develop our Leadership Academy, but, above all, he was a gifted Bible teacher. Being from a science background, Peter was especially passionate about the creation story, so I asked him to sit down with me over a period of weeks and open up Genesis, chapter 1, for me in great detail. Later on, when touring with Third Day, I used the basis of Peter's teaching to help us look at each of the six days of creation during our devotions. Here's a snapshot of some of those devotionals.

A LESSON FROM THE ROAD

Lord of All Creation

In the beginning God created the heavens and the earth. The earth was empty, a formless mass cloaked in darkness. And the Spirit of God was hovering over its surface. Then God said, "Let there be light," and there was light. And God saw that it was good. Then he separated the light from the darkness. God called the light "day" and the darkness "night." Together these made up one day.—Genesis 1:1–5 NLT

Genesis chapter 1 is the first chapter of the first book, and right from the start, it tells us what God is like. He is present from the very beginning; in fact He is there before the beginning. He is outside creation, and He is eternal. We see in the very first words of the Bible that God is creative! He makes things, and He makes those things out of nothing! The Hebrew language also tells us that God can make things out of stuff already there. When the words "made" and "created" are used later on in Genesis 1, they mean something slightly different from the "created out of nothing" in verse 1. Out of nothing God created the heavens and the earth. His raw material was empty and formless, and then He went about shaping it. His Spirit "hovered" over the surface, displaying God's protection and care. On the fourth day of creation we read a small phrase that is given almost as an afterthought: "He also made the stars" (Genesis 1:16 NLT).

Astronomers will be able to tell us just how much is packed into that small phrase! It's actually impossible to count the stars. If we could count three million stars a second, it would still take us over ten million years to count all the stars! That's the enormity of creation carried in the small phrase tucked away at the end of Genesis 1:16.

Throughout the Bible we see an emphasis on "new creation," "new thing," and God being able to "make all things new." He carries on with His creativity for all time. During the creation story, we read about the height of God's creative process:

So God created people in his own image;
God patterned them after himself;
male and female he created them.—Genesis 1:27 NLT

Being made in the image of God means that we inherit the creative characteristic of the Lord of all creation. God meant us to be creative too. Throughout God's own creative process, He constantly stepped back, took delight in what He had created, and saw that it was good. When we pause to consider the significance of God creating human beings, the following points jump out to us:

- We are on God's agenda! We are important to Him.
- We read four times in verses 26 and 27 that God created us in His image, so it must be especially important. We are the visible representation of God on earth.

- We have divine authority on earth. Ancient Roman coins carried an image of Caesar on them, giving them authority as valid currency. God's image gives us authority, fully discovered in the new covenant of Jesus Christ.
- We have been filled with the breath, the life, and the Spirit of God.

The very first words God utters to man in Genesis 1:28 are commands to be fruitful, to be in control of the living creatures on the earth. In other words, He was saying, "Be creative." So God's creative spark is within us, His command to us is to be creative, and it's up to us to discover the God-given creativity within us and use it fruitfully.

Being the main lyricist, more of the credit and the pressures for Third Day's creativity fall on Mac Powell. I've always been fascinated by the song-writing process, probably because I've never written one in my life. Mac explains how he approaches writing a new song.

It's not easy for me to write songs. Even though I love to write, it doesn't come naturally to me; I have to work at it. Even now I hear songs on the radio and think, "I wish I could have written that!" I'm proud of the songs I've written, but I believe there is still much more to come. The fun part of being in a band is to share ideas with each other, to bounce those ideas around, to encourage each other with those ideas. What's not always so fun is that you get the straight truth back when you share song ideas. Someone will say it's not great. That's difficult to take, but it helps with the process. There have been a few songs I've written and thought were good, but they didn't make the grade with the rest of the band. Once or twice other band members have come to me with a song that at first

I didn't think was very good, but we've worked on it, and by the end of the process, I can see that it's a great song. We've all had what we thought were great ideas that didn't pan out.

We often get credit for our originality, but I'm not sure we are so original because most of the strong lyrical ideas we have are copied straight from the Bible. I look to Scripture for lyrical inspiration, especially for our worship songs. Then as a band, we are creative with the music we put around the lyrics. For example, for "My Hope Is You," I sat down and read Psalm 25, thinking it would be a great idea for a song, and asking, "How can I write down those words lyrically?" That's very typical of how our song lyrics start.

To a certain degree, in the studio we all have a say in what goes on. For example, because my guitar playing is limited, I can't always demonstrate or even explain where I want a song to go, so the other guys take hold of it and take it to a better place than I could have imagined. Then there are times when I hear someone else's song and I have an idea where it should go musically, so I throw that into the mix, and we discuss it. The process can be tiring and hard work, but it's also fun, and we really enjoy it.

Mac Powell, November 2006

Mac isn't the only songwriter in the band, however. He's taken us through the general process, so let's allow Brad Avery and Mark Lee to describe to us the thought processes about some of the songs they have written.

—EAGLES—

I will soar on the wings of eagles
I will learn to fly high above this
world

BRAD

Sometimes we find ourselves fighting life's battles with both arms tied behind our backs. Yet determined not to back down, we trudge on headfirst into war. We forget our enemy's weakness; and we battle on foot, on his turf, and by his rules. Eventually we are driven to our knees and unable to pull ourselves up. God never intended it to be this way. He created us to soar like eagles. Why? Eagles fly higher than their enemies and build their nests far out of the reach of their predators. Eagles are equipped with two sets of eyelids, one of which functions like sunglasses. When being chased by their enemy, they fly straight into the direction of the sun, blinding their predator. When being pursued by our opponent, we too should soar higher, straight toward the Son. I love how melancholy the song begins, with a mood and texture like the theme of M*A*S*H* . It leaves the listener searching and wondering before busting wide open with hope and renewed energy. This song has an infectious groove, compliments of Tai's ferocious bass pulse. Don't be afraid to turn up the subwoofer.

Brad Avery

—I CAN FEEL IT—

I seek the silence through the chaos
and the noise
That's when I'm listening; I want to
hear Your voice
Sometimes it softly speaks, a whisper
on the wind
Sometimes it's louder when Your Spirit rushes in

Song ideas can come from all kinds of different places. Some of my favorites have been those that have been sparked by conversation. The idea for "I Can Feel It" came from a conversation I was having with some friends about the Holy Spirit. One of them was sharing about how he's seen the Spirit show up in different ways at different times. This was one of those concepts that didn't quite make sense to me at first, but on thinking about it, it had to make sense. This song reflects my desire to be sensitive to the Holy Spirit to the point that I can both feel Him showing up and also sense how He's showing up. I look forward to playing this one live because it can serve as a cool invocation for the Holy Spirit to come down and be a part of our show.

It's interesting that an old-school Pentecostal song like "I Can Feel It" can appear on the same record as a more liturgical song like "Communion."

MARK

This goes along with the message of unity we've been talking about since the *Come Together* days. We come from different denominational backgrounds and traditions. Rather than bicker about those differences, we can learn from each other and be the body of Christ we are called to be. Musically, this song reminds me of something we would have done ten years ago. It's kind of cool to get to the point where you can rip yourself off.

Mark Lee

-SHOW ME YOUR GLORY-

I caught a glimpse of Your splendor
In the corner of my eye
The most beautiful thing I've ever seen
And it was like a flash of lightning
Reflected off the sky
And I know I'll never be the same

For a few years I had wanted to write a song about the transfiguration. Jesus had been going along with His disciples, healing people, and in the middle of all that you have Him going up a mountain with Peter, James, and John. Elijah is there, Moses is there, and God is there. It's a big thing that's happening! In Peter's second letter he describes how this event gave him the encouragement to go on and do what he did—that's so cool.

MARK

We did not follow cleverly invented stories when we told you
about the power and coming of our Lord Jesus Christ, but
we were eyewitnesses of his majesty. For he received honor
and glory from God the Father when the voice came to him
from the Majestic Glory, saying, "This is my Son, whom I love;
with him I am well pleased." We ourselves heard this voice
that came from heaven when we were with him on the sacred
mountain.—2 Peter 1:16–18 NIV

I wanted to talk about the glory of God and the splendor of God. I had
the verses of the song worked out but couldn't fit in the chorus. Then I
found another great thing in the Bible when the notes in the margin sent
me to Exodus where Moses had a similar mountaintop experience. It's
the spot where God is laying out His plans for Moses and Moses says,
"Show me your glory" (Exodus 33:18 NIV).

God says to Moses that He won't be able to let him see His face, but
that He will let His glory pass by. So Moses sees God in all His glory and
splendor. That must have changed his life completely. All of us Christians have experienced that in a small way when Jesus comes into our
lives, just like He did with the apostle Paul. We meet God, and in that
one instant we see God in His splendor, and He completely transforms
the rest of our lives. We then want to live our lives for Him and not for
ourselves.

There is a cool line in the second verse that talks about coming back
down the mountain and not settling for ordinary things. That idea was
inspired by my uncle, an evangelist who was just back from a missionary
trip to India. While he was there, he saw a group of missionaries setting
out on foot to China. He asked someone near him when the missionaries would be coming back. He replied, "What are you talking about?
They're not going to come back. They are missionaries, and they are
going to die in China as missionaries." When my uncle returned to his

regular meetings in Atlanta, he thought to himself, "This is silly! I can't do these meetings after seeing what I've seen." We have experiences when we see God at work in our lives or in the lives of others, and we don't want to settle for the regular things in life anymore. We want to seek after the things of God for the rest of our lives.

It's great to write a song that says so many different things. On one level it's personal—I had that experience when I came to know Jesus—but it's also about Peter and Moses and partly inspired by my uncle. It's about all these things, yet it makes sense. The second verse talks about coming down the mountain, but until then you don't realize that it's set on a mountain. I just jotted down a load of ideas for the song that I had collected over a long period and didn't really know what I was going to do with them. A couple of days later it all came together when I wrote it out. In one way, it took an hour to write, and in another way, it took two years.

When I was writing it, I thought that even if it's just for me, I'm cool with that, but I played it to the other guys, and they liked it, so it went on the record. At the time I was actually trying to write rock songs because we had done most of the *Time* album and needed one or two rock songs for it. I played a few rock song ideas to the band before I played "Show Me Your Glory," but when everyone liked it, we recorded it.

It features in our set as a transition between the rocks songs and the worship songs, and by singing it, we are saying, "Tonight we want You to be here, Lord. We can't go on unless You are present." It's our cry to Jesus, saying we want to include Him completely in all His glory. The first time we played it live there was a big tough security guy in front of the stage who was supposed to be keeping the crowd in line. He was singing along and crying. I almost started crying myself—I really wasn't ready for it to affect someone like that! It was so humbling to see God use a song in that way.

Mark Lee

-RISE UP-

So rise up, my friend
No, this will never be the end
So rise up, my friend
And live again

A couple of years ago, God started doing something in my life that left a permanent mark on my heart. In little more than a twelve-month span, I grieved the loss of both of my grandfathers and one of my aunts. Also, during this time, my pastor lost his father. I watched my parents wrestle through the memories and pain of the abuse they suffered as children and the abuse they suffered while ministering in the church for over twenty years. I had friends around me struggling through divorce, addictions, and financial woes. God was opening my eyes to the turmoil and hardships of His children.

I wanted to write a song that not only encouraged my loved ones and friends, but also was therapeutic for my own condition. As I was reading the Gospels one day, I came upon the story of Lazarus. He was a close friend of Jesus and the brother of Mary and Martha, and he had tragically died. The Scriptures say Jesus wept when He saw him. Mary, Martha, and their friends were distraught. They had seen Jesus perform amazing miracles, often seeing Him completely heal those who had the same infirmities their brother Lazarus eventually succumbed to. Jesus, knowing He wanted to bring glory to God, had waited until after Lazarus's death to come and heal him. He knew the impact it would make on the world as people realized that the Messiah had power over life and death.

I needed that power in my life. I wanted that power for my family and friends. We longed to be brought back to life from the depths of our grief and despair.

I tried to approach the lyrics as if Christ were speaking to the listener personally; I could think of nothing more endearing than to be referred to as a "friend of Jesus," just as Lazarus was described in Scripture. I imagined that what I was enduring emotionally was similar to what Christ and Lazarus's family must have felt that day. It was comforting to know that I was not alone; Christ was there with me in my struggle and pain. I wanted the listener to feel this same comfort. As I worked through the song's verses, I was reminded of the passage proclaiming that "nothing can separate us from the love of God." My dark cloud was suddenly pierced with a new ray of hope. This wasn't the end. The One who conquered death and was all-powerful over everything this world could dish out was at my side. He was calling me to "rise up" and "come forth," to press on and live again with the hope of eternity as my fuel for forging ahead. Christ is calling all of His friends who are burdened with heartache and bound by addiction to crawl out of the depths of despair, set our eyes on things eternal, and carry on with the comfort, peace, and expectant hope of a blessed life ahead.

Brad Avery

I don't know about you, but I've listened to many songs for years and years without discovering the meaning of the song or the reason the song was written. So to have some of my favorite Third Day songs unpacked by the writers themselves has been a real blessing. Understanding the motives of Mac, Brad, and Mark means whenever I listen to these songs now, I am ministered to at a whole new level. I hope that it is the same for you after you've read about these songs.

10

MAY YOUR WONDERS NEVER CEASE

-MAY YOUR WONDERS NEVER CEASE-

May Your wonders never cease
May Your Spirit never leave
May we ever long to see Your face
When we've turned from You again
Oh how quickly we forget
May we be reminded of Your grace
May Your wonders never cease

I used to say there were three people I'd love to meet. Billy Graham was one, and we met him when we played a Billy Graham crusade. I've always wanted to meet a president, and in 2004 we met George W. Bush when we played at a rally and he came backstage and spoke to us for five minutes or so. He knew who we were, and we had a good conversation. The third person, or rather people, I've always wanted to meet was U2. We got to meet Bono; that was very cool.

Sometimes I wake up early in the morning and reflect about my life in Third Day—all the experiences and opportunities we have had, all the people we have met, all the great musicians we have worked with in the studio, all the pinnacle moments of our career—and I think to myself, "What more could I want?" It's always a convicting moment and makes me determined to show my thankfulness more and express it to God more frequently. Everything we've wanted, we have dreamed of, has come true! I don't know why, but I thank God for it!

David Carr, November 2006

Los Angeles International Airport, January 2005: I am waiting at the United Airlines check-in desk with Jenn, our tour manager, and Geof Barkley, the keyboard player. We're about to board a flight to Australia for Third Day's tour, and each of us has an extra-large green bag full of band merchandise to check in. Rick, the band's regular merchandise manager, isn't on this tour, so I have the twin responsibilities of pastor and merchandise man! The fun really starts at the Melbourne Airport when we have to make an inventory for Australian Customs of each individual T-shirt, poster, wristband, and hat even though we have a completed list with us. Then we learn we need an Australian customs broker to legally bring our merchandise into the country. I have no option other than to go on out and attempt to contact a broker. Meanwhile, Jenn and Geof dutifully wait near piles of T-shirts; the guys are busy finding a coffee shop or checking out the price of Australian cell phones. I eventually find a customs broker who agrees to help us out, and we all fly onto Adelaide, hoping and praying that our merchandise will follow us on the next day as promised by the broker.

During the whole of our journey and the interesting experience with customs, I have been preparing myself for the great opportunity of visiting Australia and New Zealand and am contemplating what the lasting value of the tour will be.

Third Day had toured Australia and New Zealand before, but it was going to be my first time in either country. I was looking forward to visiting a relative in Adelaide, seeing Sydney Harbor, and introducing the guys to some real live cricket in one of Australia's great stadiums. I was excited about our concerts at Hillsong Church in Sydney and at the Parachute Festival in New Zealand.

In all my excitement and thinking, I was drawn toward a devotional I had read from John Maxwell's book *The 21 Most Powerful Minutes in a Leader's Day*, and I determined to use it in the first devotional time with the band.

Here's Mark Lee's memory of those first few days of the tour as recorded on the Third Day website at the time:

We connected through Melbourne and on to our first tour stop in Adelaide. Even though we were tired, there was definitely an air of excitement among our camp—this was the first time the band had been to Aussie since 2001, and for some of our crew, this was their first-ever trip to that part of the world. Most of us spent our first full day getting ourselves acclimated to the time change (translated: we went to the hotel and "crashed"). We are very fortunate to have our road pastor, Nigel, on this trip with us. Being from the United Kingdom of Great Britain, Northern Ireland, and Principality of Wales, he is a huge cricket fan. So he, Brad, Mac, and I went to the world-famous Adelaide Oval where a cricket match was in progress. Nigel did his best to show us the finer points of the game, and I think most of us really enjoyed it. Of particular interest was the cuisine featured at the cricket grounds: chips and meat pies. Very tasty! Then on the day of the concert in Adelaide, we did some sightseeing in the morning before heading over to the venue to do the show. Adelaide is a beautiful city featuring green rolling hills, a river running through the middle of town, and a magnificent cathedral. (Not to mention the cricket grounds!) Tonight's show was incredible. None of us really knew what to expect, but we were totally blown away by the warm reception we were given. Audio Adrenaline shared the bill with us. We have known those guys for a long time and are all huge fans of theirs, so it was a real treat. They totally brought the house down and even did an extended "cowbell solo" during their encore. The opening band was an Australian outfit called Rookie. I think a highlight of the evening was the study that Nigel did with the bands before the show. He challenged us to look for more than trophies or souvenirs to remember this trip. Rather, we should be looking for ways to leave a legacy. It was very encouraging.

Mark Lee

In the devotional I shared some of the thoughts from John Maxwell about Jesus leaving behind a legacy wherever He went. If you think about it, every church, every believer, every Christian band or ministry is a direct legacy of Jesus' time on earth and the results of the obedience of His followers in Bible times and throughout the centuries. This is the devotional message we looked at:

174

A LESSON FROM THE ROAD

FRUIT THAT LASTS

Jesus said this to His disciples:

You didn't choose me. I chose you. I appointed you to go and produce fruit that will last, so that the Father will give you whatever you ask for, using my name.—John 15:16 NLT

We've heard this verse many times, but have you ever wondered how you produce fruit that will last? Fruit, at first, tends not to be ready to eat, and then it is ripe for a few days, and then it quickly goes rotten unless you preserve it. As leaders coming to serve the church in Australia and New Zealand, how will we ensure that we produce fruit that lasts?

What do we want to endure from this tour? John Maxwell talks about three types of leaders and the "fruit" they want to produce. I've given each leader a name:

The selfish leader simply wants to collect souvenirs from life.

We can travel around on this tour, take photos, buy a toy koala bear, or grab a signed tour poster, but none of that will lead to a lasting kingdom impact, even though those things might remind us of our concerts.

The shallow leader is desperate to win trophies in life.

So we might take pride in a sell-out crowd in a certain city or a fantastic response to a worship time. We may think that our success can be judged on music-industry awards, number one hits, or Gold Records.

The smart or strong leader is concerned about leaving a legacy.

We can realize that true value comes from what we leave behind us and from producing fruit that lasts.

So how do we leave a legacy? We do it the same way Jesus did: by pouring ourselves into people so that they can pour their lives into others.

> For this is my blood, which seals the covenant between God and his people. It is poured out to forgive the sins of many.
> —Matthew 26:28 NLT

And we take heart from the example of the apostle Paul:

> But whatever I am now, it is all because God poured out his special favor on me—and not without results. For I have worked harder than all the other apostles, yet it was not I but God who was working through me by his grace.—1 Corinthians 15:10 NLT

> But even if my life is to be poured out like a drink offering to complete the sacrifice of your faithful service (that is, if I am to die for you), I will rejoice, and I want to share my joy with all of you.—Philippians 2:17 NLT

Let's be determined to leave behind a legacy in Australia and New Zealand that will help build the kingdom of God.

So we determined on the tour to sacrificially pour our lives into serving—not into just collecting souvenirs or trophies, but to leave behind fruit that lasts. Just to prove that the Lord has a great sense of humor, let me tell you a follow-up story about the Australia and New Zealand tour. I decided to present a "Man of the Match" award each night for the best performance by an individual in the band or crew. Man of the Match is the British sporting equivalent of the MVP. So just for fun I might choose Mac for a great comment from stage on Australia Day, or "Wheels," one of the crew, for a particularly demanding day. Mark Lee bought a yellow Australian rules football ("Australian rules" is what Australian's call their version of football), and we used that as the award. The recipients signed it on the night they won the award, and I made sure by the end of the tour that everyone had won it once! Then on our final day Mark realized that he didn't have enough space in his luggage for the ball, and he didn't want to deflate it.

Graciously, he gave it to me; but then we realized our dilemma—surely I couldn't accept it as a souvenir! Or as a trophy! So I accepted it as a permanent reminder of a successful tour and, most importantly, of the lives we had impacted in the name of Jesus.

It sits on a shelf in my office back in Cardiff, and every time I look at it I realize that Third Day leaves a powerful legacy behind them wherever they go. Fast-forward to our tour of Australia and New Zealand in early 2007 and Mark Lee's entry

on the band's weblog on Australia Day:

MARK "God bless Australia!" That's the final thing Mac said from stage tonight, and I don't think it could be said better. God bless you guys for having us in your country and being so good to us. God bless you guys on your national holiday. But most importantly, may God continue to work in the lives of believers in this country. It's been obvious to us in spending just a few days here that something special is going on in this part of the world, and it was truly an honor for us to play a small role in that this week. Since it was Australia Day, that was the theme that ran throughout the night. Revive did a rendition of "We Are One," which is sort of an unofficial Australian anthem. They even enlisted the help of Mac on the vocals. Apparently it doesn't matter if you've lived here all your life or if you're on a three-hour layover at the Sydney Airport, you're an Australian! I joke, but the culture and the attitudes here are so infectious, it doesn't take long to soak it in and feel like an Australian at heart.

In that spirit, we ditched the "Knight Rider" intro we've been using for the last several months and instead played a rousing rendition of "Advance Australia Fair" before we walked on. Yes, it was a bit of a risk, but it paid off as the whole crowd sang along. No "Back in Black" this time, but we really enjoyed starting the show this way. We said afterward that we wished we'd filmed this night for a DVD. Everything that has been great about the first two shows happened again tonight, but on a grander scale. People were singing, worshiping, and having a great time. The first three rows seemed like they might have all come together—at any rate, it was truly a joy to look out and see everyone so involved. Too bad we didn't film it. I think a DVD titled *God Bless Australia* would've been amazing. So it is with mixed feelings that we leave tomorrow for New Zealand. We're excited to play the Parachute Festival again, and it feels good to be at least heading in the general direction of home. But this Australian visit was our shortest to date, and we all wish we could have stayed longer for some sightseeing. It definitely left us wanting more, which is a good thing. We hope to be back real soon!

Mark Lee, January 2007

Without exaggerating, everyone connected with Third Day is aware that wherever the band goes, it imparts not just a great concert and awesome music but a lasting spiritual deposit in people's lives. God really is about His business through the ministry of Third Day. Brad speaks on behalf of the band when he observes this, too:

What a blessing to be part of something that is so much bigger than we could have achieved on our own. When we started out playing music together, our only desire was to be able to play in front of people and share the message of hope with whoever would listen. Of course, we were passionate about the music we were creating and wanted it to be excellent, but we were thrilled to be able to play just a few nights a week and tell our story. We knew that the story we shared was the most powerful ever to be lived, written, or told. We had witnessed this power firsthand in our own lives and wanted others to experience it also. So, we wrote songs about the gospel, our faith, and how God had rerouted our lives from a destructive path to one that leads to eternal freedom.

As our faith matured over time, so did our writing. Our message remained the same, but we discovered new ways to deliver it. We wanted to reach as many people as possible. Much like the apostle Paul, we were striving to be "all things to all people, that we might win some." That meant honing our skills even further and taking chances. Being dangerous and fresh. Speaking in a way that all might be able to understand—not just a few. Playing in venues that those who had never entered a church would feel comfortable attending.

We also wanted to give back to God in worship the honor and praise we felt He deserved, so we recorded material in a way that wasn't calculated and methodical. Instead, we relied on God to show up supernaturally, fuse our music together, and cover it with His Spirit. That time in worship moved us and challenged us to use our platform to mobilize our fans. We were convinced that vertical worship alone was empty unless it led to an outpouring and "mighty flood of justice" for the needy children of God around the world. We began pointing people to organizations that were doing the work of Christ internationally. World Vision, Habitat for Humanity, DATA, Invisible Children, and many others were being the "hands and feet" of Christ. They met basic needs and exemplified His love with the good news as their foundation and fuel. Today, the message remains the same. Yet, we will always endeavor to present it in a way that ultimately will touch the listener's heart and "spur them on to love and good deeds." We strive to make an impression on this world that is much more than artistic and cultural. We want the time we have been given to be used effectively and to make a lasting impact eternally on the lives of God's children. This is the legacy of Third Day.

Brad Avery, October 2006

On the spring leg of the *Wherever You Are* tour, we found ourselves in Los Angeles, playing at Universal Studios, when David invited me to lunch with some of the guys. We would be visiting the home of Thomas Wilson and his family. That name might mean nothing to you, but if I mention that Thomas Wilson played the bullying Biff Tannen in all the *Back to the Future* movies, then you'll probably know who I mean.

Thomas is now a musician, a standup comedian, and a strong believer. As well as serving us with a good lunch and being a very amusing host, Thomas also showed us his den. It's the place where he paints, writes, and listens to music. It's also the place where he keeps a few select mementos from the *Back to the Future* films—one of the hover boards, for example. We talked a little bit about the impact of those films and whether he felt frustrated to always be remembered for being in them. "On the contrary," replied Thom, "it was and still is a privilege." He was proud to include the *Back to the Future* movies in his list of achievements. For many of us there that day, it was a surreal experience because we'd all seen the movies when we were younger, and here we were talking to one of the stars. It was yet another instance when we paused to consider the impact of popular culture and the opportunity to shape and influence people's lives.

Mac reflects on Third Day's effect and the things he is most proud to have left as a lasting legacy.

Winning five Dove Awards, including Band of the Year and Artist of the Year, sticks out in my mind. To this day I still can't give an acceptance speech for an award without being amazed that it is happening and without crying and shaking. I get so nervous and excited thinking that our peers have acknowledged us. Then we go backstage and high-five each other! Our times at the Grammy Awards have been special too, but for me the most emotional and memorable times have been the Doves because those are our people, our peers, and our friends in our industry. When I hear someone singing a Third Day song in church or at an event, or I hear one of our songs on the radio, I'm still, even today, as excited by that as the first time I experienced it. When we receive an award or get a number one single, I'm still very excited and never take those things for granted.

As I look back on our time together, I'm very proud that we have been the same five guys together since 1994. That's a big deal for me—and that we've remained faithful to our calling and to the music we believe we should be playing. Our catalog of music has been the thing that has most affected people. Not the Dove Awards, or the Gold Records, or our videos, but it's the songs that God has used to affect people's lives. That's what I'm most proud of.

Mac Powell, November 2006

I'm writing my final piece for this book in my own study, a couple of weeks after Third Day's successful tour of the UK in May 2007.

The guys flew over to London straight after being on a Christian music cruise for a week and, with just twenty-four hours rest, went into a hectic UK schedule. Our itinerary went like this:

Sunday: regroup and rest in a London hotel, with an early evening devotional time.

Monday: play at the Royal Albert Hall, London, for an HIV/AIDS charity benefit concert.

Tuesday: travel down to Cardiff for a concert in the night-club venue at Cardiff University.

Wednesday: day off, visit Stonehenge and then Oxford on a C. S. Lewis tour.

Thursday: fly to Belfast, Northern Ireland, for a concert in Northern Ireland's largest church.

Friday: fly to Glasgow to perform in Barrowlands, a legendary rock 'n' roll club.

Saturday: fly home! The band back to Atlanta, the crew back to Nashville, me back to Cardiff.

Four completely different performance venues in a whistle-stop tour of all four nations of Great Britain, with some typically British sightseeing thrown in the middle! It's always exciting for me to work with Third Day in the UK, and this tour was no different. Perhaps a personal highlight was being able to sleep in my own bed on the night of the Cardiff concert. Now that was a first! Sleeping in my own house in the middle of a Third Day tour! It felt very strange—the last time we played Cardiff, we drove overnight to the next concert, but this time the guys stayed in a Cardiff hotel.

Reflecting on the tour has given me the opportunity to sum up what I believe Third Day's ministry is all about, why I am committed to partnering with them, and what I believe they will ultimately be remembered for. Just hours after the band landed in London, I wandered down to the famous "Speakers Corner" in Hyde Park with Tai and a couple of crew guys. Speakers Corner is a place where anyone can come along, stand on a box or a stepladder, and begin speaking out or preaching. Many people go to speak, and even more go along to listen. In years gone by some of London's finest preachers would be there on a Sunday afternoon, but now it's a cosmopolitan selection of folks that can be found there—numerous Christian evangelists, Muslims of different groups and perspectives, Rastafarians, one or two die-hard Communists, humanists, atheists, and one or two plain eccentrics!

We wandered around for a while, just watching and listening to the various speakers competing with each other for the crowd's attention. Some members of the crowd would heckle and shout out in disagreement, and some of the speakers would engage each other directly in argument. It reminded me of the marketplace the apostle Paul visited in Athens in Acts 17.

While we were wandering around, Tai made a very perceptive comment, which he's liable to do from time to time. He noticed that some of the world's big questions were being debated right there in the open air in a London park. Christians and Muslims, in particular, were engaged in heated debate. I made the observation that this phenomenon was unlikely to be seen anywhere else in the world. People would either be moved on for creating a public nuisance or be arrested by the government for blasphemy. Something sparked inside Tai, perhaps when he couldn't resist joining in the dialogue, but he was challenged by the scene and realized that this was the world that Third Day was called to be witnesses in.

There was very little theology we would have disagreed with spoken by the Christians present, but the way they presented their faith wasn't exactly seasoned with grace, compassion, or mercy. As we walked away from the scene, Dave, Third Day's production manager, reckoned the most effective Christian presence he had experienced at Speakers Corner was from a small, elderly man who simply walked around placing his hand on people's shoulders and telling them that God loved them.

A couple of hours later in our Bible study together, which focused on building our faith for the concerts ahead, Tai and I shared some of our feelings about Speakers Corner. We said it reminded us all that, in the modern-day melting pot of ideas, ideals, and ideologies, Third Day has a significant part to play as witnesses and communicators of the God who wants to reach out to everyone with the touch of His Son Jesus and say, "I love you."

The four concerts in the UK that week certainly demonstrated the powerful ministry of Third Day, with the audiences enjoying a rock show and experiencing a powerful encounter with the Lord. It was a privilege for me, in Cardiff, Belfast, and Glasgow, to spend some time talking to the audience each night about two overseas projects we were encouraging the crowd to help us with. Ignite has been building churches in India in the poorest villages near the school Third Day helped to fund; and Trevor King from Belfast, who helped us promote the UK concerts, has been supporting a project in Ghana that is rescuing children from slavery in the fishing industry. We raised over £9,000 from the three concerts, which is about $18,000. In the Barrowlands venue, a notorious rock venue in a very rough part of Glasgow, the bar was open during the concert, and as the buckets went around for people to donate money, the bar staff collected up all their tips and donated them to the projects. When we discovered this, we were both thrilled and humbled at the same time.

These were four concerts out of the thousands over the years that the band has played, but they were four concerts that epitomized exactly who Third Day is. Not that the band is finished by any means, but the legacy they will leave is as a massively accomplished rock band, a bunch of worshipers who lead others into life-changing encounters with God, and members of the body of Christ who serve the body worldwide and who encourage the body to reach out in Christian love to those who are desperately in need.

COPYRIGHT INFO FOR SONG LYRICS

1

—CONSUMING FIRE—

Lyrics by Mac Powell c.1995 Vandura 2500 Songs (ASCAP) (admin. by EMI CMG Publishing)/New Spring (ASCAP).

2

—ROCKSTAR—

Lyrics by Mac Powell c.2004 Consuming Fire Music (ASCAP) All rights administered by EMI Christian Music Publishing.

—HOW DO YOU KNOW—

Lyrics by Mac Powell c.2005 Consuming Fire Music (AS-CAP) All rights administered by EMI CMG Publishing.

3

—COME TOGETHER—

Lyrics by Mac Powell c.2001 New Spring Publishing, Inc./ Vandura 2500 Songs/(ASCAP). All rights administered by Brentwood-Benson Music Publishing, Inc.

—CRY OUT TO JESUS—

Lyrics by Mac Powell c.2005 Consuming Fire Music (AS-CAP) All rights administered by EMI CMG Publishing.

4

—COME ON BACK TO ME—

Lyrics by Mac Powell c.2004 Consuming Fire Music (AS-CAP) All rights administered by EMI Christian Music Publishing.

5

—SING A SONG—

Lyrics by Mac Powell c.2003 Consuming Fire Music (ASCAP).

6

—CRY OUT TO JESUS—

Lyrics by Mac Powell c.2005 Consuming Fire Music (ASCAP) All rights administered by EMI CMG Publishing.

—LOVE HEALS YOUR HEART—

Lyrics by Brad Avery c.2005 Consuming Fire Music (ASCAP) All rights administered by EMI CMG Publishing.

—TUNNEL—

Lyrics by Mac Powell c.2005 Consuming Fire Music (ASCAP) All rights administered by EMI CMG Publishing.

7

—SAN ANGELO—

Lyrics by Mac Powell c.2004 Consuming Fire Music (ASCAP) All rights administered by EMI Christian Music Publishing.

—MOUNTAIN OF GOD—

Lyrics by Mac Powell and Brown Bannister c.2001 Vandura 2500 Songs (ASCAP)/New Spring, a division of Zomba Enterprises, Inc. (ASCAP). All rights for the US on behalf of Vandura 2500 Songs (ASCAP) administered by Zomba Enterprises, Inc./ Banistuci Music (ASCAP) (adm. by The Loving Company).

8

—COMMUNION—

Lyrics by Mac Powell c.2005 Consuming Fire Music (ASCAP) All rights administered by EMI CMG Publishing.

—KEEP ON SHININ'—

Lyrics by Mark Lee c.2005 Consuming Fire Music (ASCAP) All rights administered by EMI CMG Publishing.

—CARRY MY CROSS—

Lyrics by Mac Powell c.2005 Consuming Fire Music (ASCAP) All rights administered by EMI CMG Publishing.

9

—GOD OF WONDERS—

Lyrics by Steve Hindalong and Marc Byrd c.2000 Meaux Mercy/Storm Boy Music/BMI (both adm. by EMI Christian Music Publishing)/New Spring Publishing, Inc./Never Say Never Songs/ASCAP (both adm. by Brentwood-Benson Music Publishing, Inc.).

—EAGLES—

Lyrics by Brad Avery c.2005 Consuming Fire Music (ASCAP) All rights administered by EMI CMG Publishing.

—I CAN FEEL IT—

Lyrics by Mark Lee c.2005 Consuming Fire Music (ASCAP) All rights administered by EMI CMG Publishing.

—SHOW ME YOUR GLORY—

Lyrics by Mark Lee, Marc Byrd, and Third Day c.2001 New Spring Publishing, Inc./Vandura 2500 Songs/ASCAP (adm. by Brentwood-Benson Music Publishing, Inc.)/Meaux Mercy/BMI (adm. by Meaux Music).

—RISE UP—

Lyrics by Brad Avery c.2005 Consuming Fire Music (ASCAP) All rights administered by EMI CMG Publishing.

10

MAY YOUR WONDERS NEVER CEASE

Lyrics by Mac Powell c.2003 Consuming Fire Music (AS-CAP).